AF594082

The Triple Crown Winners

The Story of America's Nine Superstar Race Horses

by
SUZANNE WILDING
and
ANTHONY DEL BALSO

Parents' Magazine Press • New York

PICTURE CREDITS

The Blood-Horse: pages 40, 56, 70, 85, 131, 140
United Press International: pages iv, 14, 16, 29, 36, 38, 53, 65, 75, 96, 104, 119, 122, 156, 172
Wide World Photos: pages 13, 14, 15, 80, 166, 167

A WORLD FAMOUS HORSE STORY Selection

Printed in the United States of America

Library of Congress Cataloging in Publication Data

Wilding, Suzanne.
The triple crown winners.

SUMMARY: Introduces the races that are part of the American Triple Crown and describes the breeding and training of the nine horses that have won this trophy.

1. Race horses—United States—Juvenile literature. 2. Triple Crown, American (Horse racing)—Juvenile literature. 3. Thoroughbred horse—Juvenile literature. [1. Horse racing. 2. Thoroughbred horse. 3. Triple Crown, American (Horse racing)] I. Del Balso, Anthony, joint author. II. Title.
SF338.W54 798′.43 74-30484
ISBN 0-8193-0813-7
ISBN 0-8193-0814-5 lib. bdg.

Contents

NOTE: Throughout the chapters that follow, terms known to racing buffs, but perhaps unfamiliar to the general reader, are fully explained in the glossary, Chapter 11.

War Admiral, fourth holder of the Triple Crown, recovered from a stumbling start to win a record 1937 victory at Belmont Park.

1
The Triple Crown

THE AMERICAN TRIPLE CROWN, awarded to the winner of the Kentucky Derby, the Preakness Stakes, and the Belmont Stakes, is the most coveted, most elusive, and most rewarding prize in American racing. The triangular silver trophy bestowed for its achievement represents the culmination of centuries of breeding, both here and abroad, to produce the speediest horse.

Equus has been raced since he was first domesticated by man. There are written records that Julius Caesar, two thousand years ago, drove racing chariots at a headlong gallop in the Roman arena. His legions invaded Britain in 55 B.C. bringing their horses with them. For the next two hundred years the Romans' North African stallions were crossed with native British mares. The Romans continued to race in England and the sport spread throughout the British Isles. The invaders left, but racing continued during the Middle Ages. Gradually, England became the cradle of the thoroughbred.

From Richard the Lion-Hearted to Elizabeth II, the British royal family has always been the foremost patron of the race horse. This royal patronage made racing ultrafashionable among the nobility and the landed gentry of England, and was indirectly responsible for the breeding of the thoroughbred.

The English knew that the fastest horses were the Arabians of North Africa and the Middle East and, in the mid-seventeenth century, three stallions were imported into England: the Darley Arabian, the Godolphin Barb, and the Byerly Turk. This was the birth of the thoroughbred, for every horse listed in the English and American stud books is descended from these three foundation sires through their sons: Eclipse, Herod, and Matchem.

In this country, informal racing came to the Virginia Colony early in the seventeenth century. The first formal races were held on the Salisbury Plain—now Hempstead, Long Island, New York—a few miles from the Belmont and Aqueduct race tracks. The track was laid out in the late 1600s by the first English governor of what had been Dutch New Amsterdam.

Racing took on an American flavor and many towns and villages on the East Coast held competitions—usually short sprints, rather than longer races requiring more formal courses. As the thirteen separate colonies became the United States, racing prospered, and today it is the largest spectator sport in the country.

Racing grew, and so did the business of breeding thoroughbreds. The modern race horse is the result of centuries of selective breeding, culminating in the ideal thoroughbred—a thousand pounds of bone and muscle, balanced on slender legs, with a chest deep enough to contain a heart and lungs equal to enormous effort. At a gallop the head and neck are outstretched, the ears are pricked forward, and the fluid stride is long and low.

This book is about the nine thoroughbred superstars who

have won the American Triple Crown. Ben Jones, the greatest trainer of all, once oversimplified the winning of this trophy by saying that all one needs is ". . . a horse that runs faster than the rest of them three times in a row." However, this horse must be the best of the approximately 25,000 colts and fillies registered each year with The Jockey Club, the keeper of the American Thoroughbred Stud Book.

Although the first Derby was in 1875, the first Preakness in 1873, and the first Belmont in 1867, the phrase Triple Crown was not heard on this side of the Atlantic until Charles Hatton, a racing writer for the *Morning Telegraph*, used it in the 1930s.

The American Triple Crown was thus born on a reporter's typewriter, though it was named after the English Triple Crown of the Epsom Derby, the St. Leger, and the Two Thousand Guineas. Hatton picked the Kentucky Derby, the Preakness, and the Belmont for the Triple Crown, but the trio could as easily have been any other combination of important races.

From then on the Triple Crown was identified with these three races and, although still only a name, owners and trainers began to point their horses at this particular trio of prestigious three-year-old classics. Calumet Farm's Whirlaway, Mrs. John D. Hertz's Count Fleet, the King Ranch's Assault, and Calumet's Citation won in the forties, but their crowns were made of newspaper and their reigns had no official recognition.

In 1950 the Thoroughbred Racing Associations decided to award a Triple Crown trophy retroactively to each winner, from Sir Barton, who won in 1919, to Citation, in 1948. A triangular silver cup, its sides symbolizing the three races, was designed by Cartier, the famous jeweler, and nine trophies were ordered. At the Thoroughbred Racing Associations' awards dinner in 1950, the presentation was made for Sir Barton, and at subsequent yearly dinners seven additional awards were presented. Cartier's ninth trophy, which had been held in waiting for twenty-three years, did not go to Secretariat. The T.R.A. directors felt that number nine, which had been in Saratoga's National Museum of Racing or on the road all over the United States, looked a little tired and dented. They ordered a spanking new one for Secretariat. In 1973, for the first time, the T.R.A. gave small replicas of the trophy to the winning trainer and jockey as well.

The history of the Triple Crown is tied to the development of stakes races in the United States. In 1872, Colonel M. Lewis Clark, president of the Louisville Jockey Club, of Louisville, Kentucky, visited England and France to study their classic races. His ambition was to restore to the South the racing which had been ruined by the War Between the States. Yearlings of the bluest blue blood were selling for $100 and Kentucky stud farms were in bankruptcy. As a result of his trip, the Kentucky Derby was born and was run on the Louisville Jockey Club's course, purchased from the Churchill family and—much later—named Churchill Downs.

Colonel Clark died in 1899 and shortly thereafter another Kentucky colonel, Matt Winn, took over. As a boy of thirteen, he had seen his first Derby from the infield, atop his father's farm wagon. As a middle-aged man, Matt Winn gave up a successful career in tailoring to become a giant in racing promotion. He died in 1949, and the Derby has continued to prosper.

In 1875, a crowd of 10,000 saw Aristides defeat the great Ten Broeck to win the first Kentucky Derby with a $1,000-added purse. In 1973, when Secretariat ran the fastest Derby ever, 130,000 spectators flooded Churchill Downs to bet more than $3 million and to cheer him as he wore the winner's blanket of red roses.

Thanks to TV, the Derby today is "the greatest two minutes in sports." Churchill Downs, with its twin-spired grandstand, mint juleps, and the haunting notes of "My Old Kentucky Home," has become an American institution. The glamour and publicity of the Derby has helped all stakes races, especially the Preakness and the Belmont.

The Preakness Stakes, run at Pimlico Race Course, Baltimore, Maryland, is the second leg of the Triple Crown, and the richest of the three races. The first Preakness was run in 1873 for $2,050, and in 1877 Congress adjourned for the day to attend the race. Since then the purses have increased enormously; by 1973 it was $150,000 added.

In 1860, the unbelievably ornate silver Woodlawn Vase was created by Tiffany and Company as a racing trophy for the old Woodlawn Racing Association in Kentucky. The vase had been buried for safekeeping during the Civil War and returned to racing after hostilities ceased. From then on, the Woodlawn trophy was donated for a number of different races at a variety of tracks until, in 1917, it found a permanent home at Pimlico and became an added reward for crossing the finish line first in the grueling one-and-three-sixteenths-mile Preakness. The vase, until 1953, remained in the possession of the winning Preakness owner for one year. When Native Dancer won, however, Mrs. Alfred Gwynne Vanderbilt did not wish to be responsible for a $500,000 trophy. Since that time, a half-sized replica is awarded the winning owner on a permanent basis, and the Woodlawn Vase stays in Baltimore.

The weather vane on the infield cupola roof is unique with

Pimlico; it is in the form of a horse and jockey whose racing silks are painted in the colors of the previous year's Preakness winner. While the horses are still pounding down the homestretch, a track employee is perched on a stepladder, ready to paint on the winning owner's colors the moment the race's outcome is declared official.

The victorious horse is draped with a blanket of black-eyed susans. But, as black-eyed susans are not plentiful in May, a Baltimore florist each year takes thousands of daisies and dyes their centers black with shoe polish. A case of champagne is always sent to the winning horse's barn.

The Belmont Stakes, at Belmont Park, Long Island, New York, is the oldest, the longest, and the final race for the Triple Crown. First run in 1867, it was slated to be one and one-half miles, the same as the Epsom Derby in England. But, until Belmont Park opened in 1905, the race was run at other tracks and at various distances. Since 1926, when it was won by Man o'War's son, Crusader, the great American classic has become a fixture at Belmont, run over the traditional one and one-half miles.

Today's Belmont Park is a modern racing plant designed to extract the maximum number of dollars from the maximum number of people in the minimum length of time. Still, much of the old charm has been preserved. The tree-shaded walking ring is one of the most beautiful in the world, and the stable area, with its row upon row of wooden barns and white trainers' cottages, is a carryover from the bygone era when horses traveled by train, and when a day at the races was a pleasure rather than big business.

August Belmont I won the Belmont Stakes with Fenian in

1869; August Belmont II opened Belmont Park in 1905 and, in 1926, the Belmont family donated Fenian's 1869 trophy as a permanent cup for the race. It is an elaborate silver bowl, supported by statues of Eclipse, Herod, and Matchem—the three great foundation sires. The winner's share of the $125,000-added purse and a small replica of the trophy are given to the owner; trophies are also presented to the trainer, jockey, exercise boy, and groom. The horse receives a floral tribute: a blanket of white carnations, which is beautiful to look at, lovely to smell, and tasty to nibble on.

The Belmont is the most prestigious race of the Triple Crown. It is longer and later—one-quarter mile longer and thirty-five days later—than the Kentucky Derby. It has often been called the executioner of Triple Crown hopefuls. In the twenty-five years before Secretariat's triumph, seven great horses came to Belmont with two legs of the Triple Crown but failed to win the third and last race.

Before the Triple Crown became established, the Derby and the Preakness had attracted different horses. Man o'War made his three-year-old debut by winning the Preakness; his owner Sam Riddle did not enter him in the Derby. Other owners ran their horses in the Derby, but were not about to bring them from Kentucky to Maryland for the Preakness. In the days before fast horse vans and equine air transport, the journey was too great, and the time too short between races.

It is only in the recent past that the dates of the three races have been fixed with intervals of two weeks between the Kentucky Derby and the Preakness, and then three weeks more to the Belmont. In 1919, Sir Barton's Derby and Preakness wins were only four days apart. In 1922, the Derby and the Preakness were run on the same day! And in Gallant Fox's year, 1930, the Preakness was eight days *before* the Derby.

With each passing year, winning the Triple Crown becomes more difficult. In 1945, when Citation was born, 5,819 thoroughbreds were foaled in the United States; now there are more than 25,000 born annually. This enormous increase in thoroughbred breeding since World War II has greatly increased the odds against winning all three races.

There is another, basic problem: historically—and regrettably—the great classic races have been for three year olds. A three year old is a growing colt with overdeveloped muscles, but with underdeveloped bones and ligaments that are often unable to withstand the jar of one thousand pounds streaking down a track at close to forty miles an hour. Most trainers feel that the three races are too long, too close together, and too early in the season. In a space of thirty-five days, starting on the first Saturday in May, a horse is asked to run one and one-quarter, one and three-sixteenths, and one and one-half miles. Add to this the twenty-five or thirty miles of breezing and galloping between races, and the result is just too much for many youngsters.

If the big money races were for four and five year olds instead, race horses would last longer. As it is, many are crippled at two. The tough ones last through their three-year-old year. Few go on to race well at four and five.

Since Sir Barton won the Triple Crown in 1919, there have been twenty-six members of "The Two-Thirds Club": winners of two legs of the trophy. Of these, Pillory and Man o'War did not run in the Kentucky Derby; two others, Burgoo King and Bold Venture were not entered in the Belmont.

But there were other notable horses in "The Two-Thirds Club" who, except for bad luck or injury, might have achieved racing immortality. In 1953 Native Dancer became the first equine TV personality; the country fell in love with "The Gray Ghost." Out of twenty-two races, he lost only one—but that was the big one, the Kentucky Derby. Hit and almost knocked down by another horse, he still came in second to Dark Star, losing by only a head.

Tim Tam, in 1958, carried the Calumet Farm devil's red and blue silks to convincing victory in the Derby and the Preakness. A favorite for the Belmont, he lost to Irish-bred Cavan. It was a glorious defeat, because only Tim Tam's thoroughbred heart kept him going—he had broken a bone in his foot and finished on three legs. He never raced again.

Then, in 1961, came Carry Back, "The People's Horse," who caught the public's imagination with a "stretch kick." He won the Derby and the Preakness and arrived at Belmont in a shower of press clippings. Favored for the Belmont Stakes, he did not win and cooled out sore.

In 1971 Canonero II also became a member of "The Two-Thirds Club" at Belmont, where 82,694 people had turned out hoping to see him win. Bred in Kentucky, he had been sold to a Venezuelan, and in the eyes of New York's large Latino population, represented all of Latin America. He had won the Derby and set a track record for the Preakness. Every New Yorker was convinced that here, at last, was *their* Triple Crown winner. But it was not to be, for the killing pace of the three races took its toll. Canonero II faded, not only in the race, but out of racing. It took a full year for his recovery, and never again did he show his Derby and Preakness winning form.

If Riva Ridge, the 1972 Derby and Belmont winner, had not had an off day in the Preakness, Meadow Stables, the owner of both Riva Ridge and Secretariat, would have won two Triple Crowns in a row. This would have been an all-time first, and probably an all-time last.

Other stables have had both a Triple Crown winner and a near-miss. The King Ranch's Assault won in 1946 but his stablemate and half brother, Middleground, won two out of three, losing the Preakness in 1950. Whirlaway, in 1941, and Citation, in 1948, were both Triple Crown winners, but when Tim Tam lost the 1958 Belmont, he also lost Calumet Farm's chance of being the only triple Triple Crown winner.

No filly has come close to winning the Triple Crown. In more than 100 years, only four have won the Preakness, two the Belmont, and only one filly, Regret, crossed the finish line first in the Derby. It may be a simple question of physical strength, but the boy horses do seem to run faster.

Woman's Lib may even have invaded the horse world, however, because from 1973 to 1975, two great European fillies, Dahlia and Allez France, dominated the classic races.

They are the greatest money-winning fillies of all time. Both American bred, racing mainly in Europe, they are engaged in a seesaw battle for monetary supremacy. They have long since passed Shuvee, whose winnings of $890,445 had made her the richest filly in history. The owners of Allez France and Dahlia, Daniel Wildenstein of Paris and Nelson Bunker Hunt of Texas, are avowedly gunning for the topmost honor, to beat Kelso's $1,977,896.

Locust Hill Farm's Ruffian, undefeated and potentially the greatest filly ever bred, was entered in a match race with Foolish Pleasure, winner of the 1975 Kentucky Derby.

The contest, on July 6, 1975, to decide whether a great filly could out-run a colt of Triple Crown caliber, ended in a tragedy of heroic proportions. During the race Ruffian broke two bones in a front leg and was humanely destroyed.

With Dahlia, Allez France, and Ruffian having shown the way, perhaps one day we shall have a filly winner of the Triple Crown.

Although no gelding has won the Triple Crown either, many have won the big races. Some colts become "rank"—difficult to ride and almost uncontrollable—and are gelded to make them more manageable. The greatest money winner of all time, Kelso, who earned almost $2 million, was a gelding. Like many thoroughbreds, Kelso matured slowly and was not entered in any of the Triple Crown races.

It takes a great horse to win any one of the three-year-old classics, but a superhorse is needed to clinch the Triple Crown. Since 1918 only nine have appeared. Owning one of these equine stars is equivalent to discovering an oil well in the stable yard. Although the victor of the Derby, the Preakness, and the Belmont receives more than $300,000 in prize money, the stud potential of the winner of any of these classics is the real "gusher."

Riva Ridge, who won two legs of the Triple Crown in 1972, was syndicated at stud for $5,000,000, while Secretariat hit the all-time record of $6,080,000. The 1974 member of "The Two-Thirds Club," Little Current, was retired for $4,000,000.

Many are royally bred, but few wear the Triple Crown. Ability, avoiding injury, and just plain racing luck all play a part in the capture of America's greatest racing trophy.

THE TWO-THIRDS CLUB

1877 CLOVERBROOK	Not entered in Kentucky Derby
1878 DUKE OF MAGENTA	Not entered in Kentucky Derby
1880 GRENADA	Not entered in Kentucky Derby
1881 SAUNTERER	Not entered in Kentucky Derby
1895 BELMAR	Not entered in Kentucky Derby
1920 MAN O'WAR	Not entered in Kentucky Derby
1922 PILLORY	Not entered in Kentucky Derby
1923 ZEV	Lost Preakness to Vigil
1931 TWENTY GRAND	Lost Preakness to Mate
1932 BURGOO KING	Not entered in Belmont
1936 BOLD VENTURE	Not entered in Belmont
1939 JOHNSTOWN	Lost Preakness to Challedon
1940 BIMELECH	Lost Kentucky Derby to Gallahadion
1942 SHUT OUT	Lost Preakness to Alsab
1944 PENSIVE	Lost Belmont to Bounding Home
1949 CAPOT	Lost Kentucky Derby to Ponder
1950 MIDDLEGROUND	Lost Preakness to Hill Prince
1953 NATIVE DANCER	Lost Kentucky Derby to Dark Star
1955 NASHUA	Lost Kentucky Derby to Swaps
1956 NEEDLES	Lost Preakness to Fabius
1958 TIM TAM	Lost Belmont to Cavan
1961 CARRY BACK	Lost Belmont to Sherluck
1963 CHATEAUGAY	Lost Preakness to Candy Spots
1964 NORTHERN DANCER	Lost Belmont to Quadrangle

1966 KAUAI KING	Lost Belmont to Amberoid
1967 DAMASCUS	Lost Derby to Proud Clarion
1968 FORWARD PASS	Received first money in Derby although finished second to Dancer's Image.
	Lost Belmont to Stage Door Johnny
1969 MAJESTIC PRINCE	Lost Belmont to Arts and Letters
1971 CANONERO II	Lost Belmont to Pass Catcher
1972 RIVA RIDGE	Lost Preakness to Bee Bee Bee
1974 LITTLE CURRENT	Lost Derby to Cannonade

TRIPLE CROWN WINNERS

1919 SIR BARTON by *Star Shoot out of Lady Sterling

Breeders– John E. Madden and Vivian A. Gooch
Owner– Commander J. K. L. Ross
Jockey– Johnny Loftus
Trainer– H. G. Bedwell

1930 GALLANT FOX by *Sir Gallahad III out of Marguerite

Breeder– Belair Stud/William Woodward, Sr.
Owner– Belair Stud/William Woodward, Sr.
Jockey– Earl Sande
Trainer– James Fitzsimmons

1935 OMAHA by Gallant Fox out of Flambino

Breeder– Belair Stud/William Woodward, Sr.
Owner– Belair Stud/William Woodward, Sr.
Jockey– Willie (Smokey) Saunders
Trainer– James Fitzsimmons, United States
Cecil Boyd-Rochfort, Great Britain

1937 WAR ADMIRAL by Man o'War out of Brushup

Breeder– Glen Riddle Farm/Samuel D. Riddle
Owner– Glen Riddle Farm/Samuel D. Riddle
Jockey– Charley Kurtsinger
Trainer– George Conway

1941 WHIRLAWAY by *Blenheim II out of Dustwhirl

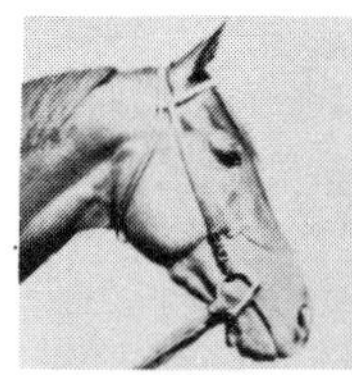

Breeder– Calumet Farm/Warren Wright, Sr.
Owner– Calumet Farm/Warren Wright, Sr.
Jockey– Eddie Arcaro
Trainer– Ben Jones

1943 COUNT FLEET by Reigh Count out of Quickly

Breeder– Mrs. John D. Hertz
Owner– Mrs. John D. Hertz
Jockey– Johnny Longden
Trainer– Don Cameron

1946 ASSAULT by Bold Venture out of Igual

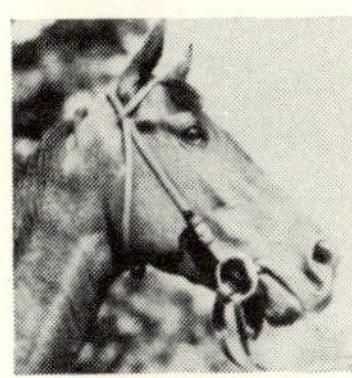

Breeder– King Ranch
Owner– King Ranch
Jockey– Warren Mehrtens
Trainer– Max Hirsch

1948 CITATION by Bull Lea out of *Hydroplane II

Breeder– Calumet Farm/Warren Wright, Sr.
Owner– Calumet Farm/Warren Wright, Sr.
Jockey– Eddie Arcaro
Trainer– Ben Jones, Jimmy Jones

1973 SECRETARIAT by Bold Ruler out of Somethingroyal

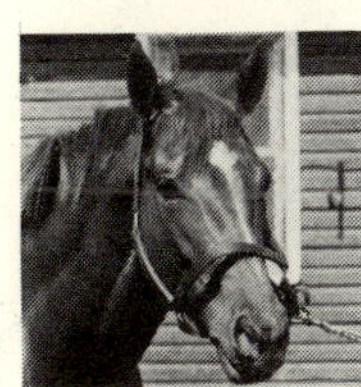

Breeder– Meadow Stud
Owner– Meadow Stable
Jockey– Ron Turcotte
Trainer– Lucien Laurin

1977 Seattle Slew
1978 Affirmed
2015 American Pharoah
2 leg winner 1981 Pleasant Colony by His Majesty out of Sun Colony
Breader-
Owner - Evans
Jockey - Jorge Velasques
Trainer - John Campo

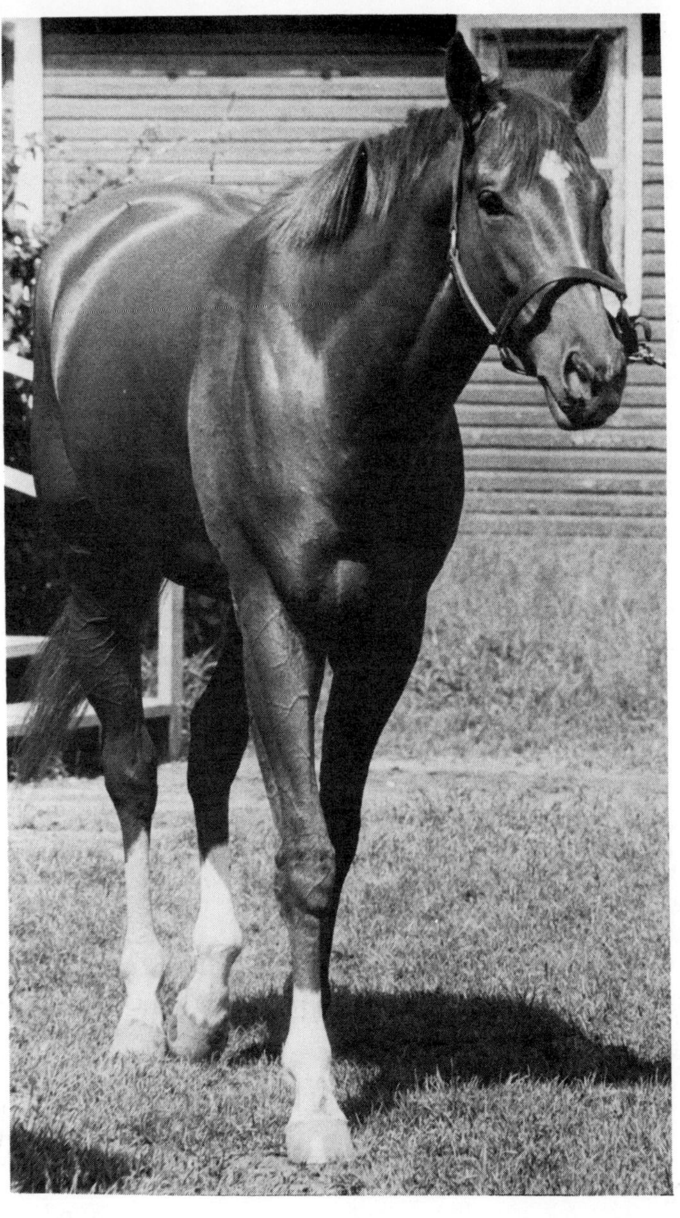

SECRETARIAT (1970–)	*BOLD RULER, 1954*		*Nasrullah*
			Miss Disco
	SOMETHINGROYAL, 1952		*Princequillo*
			Imperatrice

2

Secretariat

The Seven Million Dollar Horse

WHEN SECRETARIAT ROMPED HOME by an unheard-of thirty-one lengths in the 1973 Belmont Stakes, he became the first Triple Crown winner in twenty-five years and a symbol of equine greatness to millions of Americans. "Super Red," as his jockey, Ron Turcotte, called him, joined the ranks of such American superhorses as "Big Red"—the immortal Man o'War; Citation, the great Calumet stallion who won the Triple Crown in 1948; and Kelso, the biggest money winner of all time.

The golden chestnut and his pretty mistress, Penny Tweedy, became instant TV heroes to all America. Racing buffs loved them, and so did little old ladies from Dubuque, Iowa, who had never heard of the Big A and who thought a two-dollar bet was devil's work. In the summer of 1973, when the news was brimful of the world's problems, Secretariat and his good-looking blonde companion provided a welcome relief. Everyone shared in their triumphs.

It all started in 1936, with Mrs. Helen "Penny" Tweedy's father, Christopher T. Chenery. An engineer and self-made utilities millionaire, Chenery bought back The Meadow, his ancestral home near Doswell, in the southeast corner of Virginia. It had belonged to his family since 1810, but was lost during the Civil War.

Chenery, a poor boy from Ashland, Virginia, loved horses. As a youngster, he had worked race horses at a nearby track, but he did not have time for hobbies. Life was hard, and a good education was difficult and expensive to obtain. His older brother, William, went to college for two years and then came home so that Christopher could have his turn. They alternated in this way until Christopher T. Chenery received his engineering degree from Washington and Lee University. In 1926, he went to New York to become a consulting engineer. When he finally could afford it, he went back to his first love, horses, and he fox-hunted and played polo as hard as he worked. This interest led him to racing, and The Meadow became the sentimental home for his new stable.

Today, The Meadow with its twenty-six hundred acres is on a par with the best breeding farms in Kentucky's bluegrass country. But when Mr. Chenery first saw it, the house and paint were strangers to each other, pigs and chickens littered the yard, and the land was poor and in need of drainage and fertilization. Now the white barns trimmed in royal blue, The Meadow's racing colors, can hold their own with the best, and miles of fencing stretch as far as the eye can see. At the charming old manor house, the trophy room surpasses those in many a Lexington, Kentucky mansion.

Some call it luck, others call it skill, but over the years Chenery gathered a topnotch band of broodmares. He never had more than twenty broodmares and twenty horses in training—a small operation among the racing giants—but they were quality stock and proved their worth.

His first great mare was Hildene, an unsuccessful race horse but a superlatively successful broodmare. Bought in 1939 for $750, an absolute pittance, she raced eight times and won only $100, but she produced five colts who were stakes winners, and a pair of fillies who foaled top horses of their own.

The Chenerys usually sent their mares to studs in Kentucky and then brought them home to The Meadow. The exception was Hildene, who became blind after the birth of her first foal. She was sent back to be rebred at Claiborne Stud, the home of some of the world's top stallions, and Mr. Chenery felt it kinder to leave her there. She lived out her life as a broodmare at Claiborne, in a familiar stall and paddock with another blind mare for company.

Hildene never saw her colt, Hill Prince, the first Meadow champion. He was named top three-year-old colt and Horse of the Year in 1950, and the top four-year-old in 1951.

First Landing, another of Hildene's sons, was the leading two-year-old colt in 1958, and became the sire of Riva Ridge, Meadow Stable's 1972 Kentucky Derby and Belmont winner. Cicada, Hildene's granddaughter, was named the best filly of 1961, 1962, and 1963. She set a world record for her sex, earning $783,674, and this record stood until the brilliant Shuvee came along with $890,445.

The mare Imperatrice joined Chenery's elite band. A good broodmare, she foaled a number of stakes winners before she was bred to Princequillo, who became the champion broodmare sire for six out of seven years. The result was the filly, Somethingroyal.

Somethingroyal was something special. She produced four horses that won stakes, and three who placed. Among them was Sir Gaylord, favorite for the 1962 Kentucky Derby until his pre-race injury. At stud he became the sire of Sir Ivor, the great Kentucky-bred, English race horse.

In 1969, when Somethingroyal was seventeen years old, she was bred to Bold Ruler—and Secretariat was the product. Bold Ruler had won twenty-three races and $764,204. He became America's leading thoroughbred stallion, and is considered by many the outstanding sire of the twentieth century. Owned by Mrs. Henry Carnegie Phipps and her son, Ogden Phipps, Bold Ruler dominated racing from Box I at Claiborne Farm until he died of cancer in 1971. His most famous son, Secretariat, retired from racing to the stud farm at Claiborne and now occupies the same box stall and paddock.

Breeding is an inexact science and "Lady Luck" plays a large role, but the mating of Somethingroyal (Princequillo blood) with Bold Ruler (Nearco-Nasrullah strains) was a good mix. Bold Ruler's progeny develop early and star in short races; they are precocious and brilliant at two, and often a disappointment at three. Princequillo's sons and daughters were known as tough, late bloomers who could run forever.

The mating of a mare to a stallion—a "service"—is usually paid for in money by the owner of the broodmare. A service to Bold Ruler was harder to get than an interview with Howard Hughes and it was worth more than money; a foal, not a stud fee, was the price. A breeder was asked to send two top broodmares to Bold Ruler in two successive years; a toss of a coin was to determine first choice of the foals.

The Meadow sent two mares, Somethingroyal and Hasty Matelda, to Bold Ruler. The first crop was a filly for Somethingroyal and a colt for Hasty Matelda. The coin was tossed and, much to the Phippses' loss, they won and chose the filly. They named her The Bride. Unfortunately, she showed toward racing all the shyness and reluctance of the proverbial Victorian maiden.

The selection for the second year was The Meadow's. This proved to be academic, for Cicada, sent in Hasty Matelda's place, was barren, and Secretariat was the only choice.

Mrs. Tweedy does not remember who flipped the coin, but whoever it was did not know that there was $7,396,808 riding on the toss.

In 1968 Mr. Chenery became seriously ill and was unable to manage his business or his sporting interests. The Meadow became a ship without a rudder until his daughter Penny Tweedy took over. Although she loved to ride, and could read a balance sheet, she was not familiar with the business of running a breeding and racing establishment. She did, however, know more about business than many of her contemporaries. Penny had gone on from Smith College to win her Master's degree from the Columbia School of Business Administration. An unusual choice for a girl from a wealthy family in the 1940s.

Assisted by Elizabeth Ham, who knew the nuts and bolts of The Meadow's operation, Mrs. Tweedy managed the family racing establishment for her ailing father. The first year that she took over Meadow Stud and Meadow Stable (the breeding and racing divisions of The Meadow), they were heavily in the red, but within twelve months she managed to show a profit.

"Mrs. Tweedy has done just great, taking over the farm since her Dad got too ill to care for it," says Howard Gentry, farm manager at The Meadow for the past twenty-eight years.

With the help of the late "Bull" Hancock, she made some far-reaching decisions, the best of which was to breed Somethingroyal to Bold Ruler. As for the racing end, a stable can't do much better than to win the Derby and the Belmont one year (with Riva Ridge in 1972), and to make a clean sweep of the Triple Crown the next.

According to *Newsweek* magazine, at a 1969 family business meeting, Mrs. Tweedy's brother, Dr. Hollis T. Chenery, chief economist for the World Bank, wondered whether it wouldn't be better to sell the horses and put the money in the stock market. Another sister, Mrs. Margaret Carmichael, was also in a quandary, but it was decided that their father would not have wanted to sell the horses. A source close to the family, however, categorically denies that selling the horses was ever considered at that meeting, but it does make a good story.

Assisted by Riva Ridge and Secretariat, Mrs. Tweedy made much more money in the racing game than would have been the case if the assets of Meadow Stable had been converted into Xerox and IBM stock. Counting the two horses' winnings and their stud syndication, the total on the plus side of the ledger for The Meadow is $13,718,305. But Penny Tweedy has done much more. Aided by TV, she has brought the best of big-time racing into millions of American homes. With her ready smile and pleasant manner, she wears the title of first lady of racing with style, and follows in the footsteps of another great lady of the turf, Mrs. Ambrose Clark, who said, "When you win, look as if you are used to it; when you lose, look as though you like it."

Secretariat was born on March 30, 1970, in the foaling shed, not far from the manor house at The Meadow. He was a sassy chestnut colt with three white stockings, a white star on his forehead, and a long connecting stripe down his nose. Even then, the son of Somethingroyal had something special, for when Penny Tweedy saw him for the first time, bucking and playing in the pasture with the other colts, she wrote only one word next to his name in her notebook, and that was "Wow!!" During the following year, Howard Gentry, farm manager, told Lucien Laurin, who was busy training top two-year-old Riva Ridge, "We've got an even better one on the farm."

Meadow colts run with their dams until weaning time. In September or October of their first year, they are separated from their mothers and, after a day or so of whinnying and carrying on, they go back to nibbling grass and playing tag with the other high-priced colts and fillies.

In August of their yearling year, primary school begins on the farm. The colts are broken to saddle and bridle, worked on the training track with the other youngsters, and introduced to that monster, the starting gate. Upon graduation, they are sent to trainer Lucien Laurin at Belmont Park for high school and college. Laurin approves of their basic education, saying ". . . when the farm manager, Mr. Howard Gentry, sends horses to the track, he always sends them in fantastic shape. These are people who know how to raise race horses."

Roger Laurin, Lucien's son, had been the trainer for Meadow Stable, but in 1971 when Eddie Neloy, Ogden Phipps's trainer, died, Roger was invited to manage the much larger Phipps operation. Roger resigned from Meadow Stable and suggested his father, Lucien, to Mrs. Tweedy. The elder Laurin was planning to take Mrs. Laurin to Europe on their first real vacation in years but, instead, he canceled the trip and took over the Meadow Stable string. He has never worked harder, nor more successfully.

Lucien Laurin, son of a French-Canadian paper-mill hand, was raised in the province of Quebec. A horse crazy youngster, small enough to become a jockey, Laurin apprenticed himself to Rosaire La Croix, an owner and trainer. He started riding in 1928, "broke his maiden" (won his first race) in 1929, and although he says that he wasn't the greatest of riders, Laurin did well at the Canadian tracks. He also rode in the United States but, like almost all jockeys, weight became an ever increasing problem. In 1940, he gave up trying to win the "battle of the bulge" and became a trainer.

He started modestly on the leaky roof circuit but made it to Belmont by 1946 as a public trainer. Today, Barn Five and its adjoining tree-shaded cottage are Lucien Laurin's headquarters, and a large white sign reminds visitors that Secretariat and Riva Ridge lived there.

Over the years, Laurin trained many good horses. His first big winner was Reginald Webster's Quill, champion two-year-old filly in 1958, who earned $386,041 by the end of her racing career. In 1966 he trained Webster's Amberoid to win the Wood Memorial and the Belmont Stakes. Claiborne's Dike was another of Laurin's top horses, but he had the misfortune to be foaled the same year as two other great colts—Majestic Prince, who won the 1969 Kentucky Derby, and Arts and Letters, who finished ahead of Dike in the Run for the Roses.

Now gray-haired, chubby and volatile, Lucien Laurin is a small man who, despite his Gallic temperament, has handled the trials and tribulations of training two champions with the just right combination of savoir faire, modesty, and fatalism. He readily agrees with Jimmy Jones, trainer of the fabled Citation, who used to say that he couldn't wait to get to the barn in the morning to see his champion. Laurin felt the same way about Secretariat while he was in residence at Barn Five.

A little older, a little heavier, and much richer, Lucien Laurin plans to take it easier. Always a public trainer, he hopes to turn some of the horses over to his son, Roger. Lucien Laurin may never have another Triple Crown winner, but Meadow Stable has some good youngsters, and it won't be too long before Secretariat's first crop of foals come to the track.

Secretariat arrived at Belmont in the spring of his two-year-old year. He was still a baby, but he was a big, beautiful baby. A lustrous chestnut, he stood 16.2 hands high and was still growing. He looked like a young, conformation show horse rather than a hardworking race horse; as he developed, one columnist wrote, "Secretariat has met almost everyone's standard for excellence." A "Mr. America" among horses, he has a classic head with a broad forehead and a fine muzzle, accentuated by the white star and stripe. Beautifully put together, he combines powerful hindquarters with a chest so wide and deep that a special girth was needed to encircle his seventy-five-and-three-fourths-inch frame.

In 1972, Riva Ridge was the big name around Barn Five, but that didn't bother Secretariat. He enjoyed his routine of eating, sleeping, and early morning workouts, especially the eating. He was what horsemen call a "good doer" and would—and could—eat everything in sight. Sixteen quarts of oats and plenty of hay, carrots, vitamins, and minerals were his ration, and he ate them all. He liked to vary his meal with a few mouthfuls of oats, then a sip of water to clear his palate, then a few chews of hay. A neat eater, Secretariat always tidied up the floor by picking up stray kernels of oats and wisps of hay. By some, he was called "the neatest glutton at the track."

Big colts break down more easily than little fellows, and Lucien Laurin took no chances. He worked him slowly, not pushing him too hard and not overstraining the delicate thoroughbred legs. The red colt liked to gallop, but he was happy to be part of the gang and, during workouts, amiably let every two-bit horse on the track pass him.

"He's just too beautiful to run," was Lucien Laurin's sad comment.

During training sessions in June of his two-year-old year, he suddenly caught on to the racing game. To run with the other colts was fine, but to beat them by a nose, a head, or, even better, by several lengths, was his heritage. Once learned, this lesson was never forgotten, and on July 4, 1972, Secretariat came out on the track at Aqueduct to run in his maiden race.

Mrs. Tweedy was there, and so was Miss Elizabeth Ham for whom the colt was named. This able lady, for many years Mr. Chenery's executive secretary, now runs the Chenery Estate office in New York, is an executrix of the Estate, a partner in the Meadow Stud, and has her finger on the pulse of the whole Chenery operation.

Everything happened to Secretariat in his first race. He shot out of the gate like a seasoned campaigner, only to be bumped by a horse named Quebec. Shaken by the impact, he was hit again by a colt named Strike The Line, and if that wasn't enough, Big Burn walloped him. Secretariat ducked and dropped back; this rough stuff was too much for even a big brave colt. Way out of contention, his jockey pulled him together and, like a true son of Bold Ruler, he closed with a rush in the last quarter mile and came in a miraculous fourth.

His maiden race was the only time in his entire racing career that Secretariat was ever unplaced, and he crossed the finish line first with almost boring regularity in his next eight two-year-old races.

In speaking of the Sanford Stakes at Saratoga in August, Ron Turcotte, his jockey, described seeing a gap which began to close in front of Secretariat. "It was too late for me to take up, so I gunned my colt and he moved on through . . . I had never been on such a bold colt. . . ." In the Hopeful, his next race: ". . . I asked him to run at the half-mile pole and he made the greatest move I'd ever seen by a two year old. . . . Now I was beginning to think this colt was the best youngster I had ever ridden."

Secretariat had never felt the whip, and when Ron Turcotte used it in the prestigious Champagne Stakes at Belmont, Secretariat ducked, bearing in on Stop the Music. Although he came in first by two lengths, he was put down to second place for interfering.

During 1972, Secretariat raced at five different tracks in three states; it did not matter whether the going was hard and fast, soft and slow, or wet and muddy. He was first in all but his maiden race, and as Gene Schwartz, the clocker at Belmont, said, "He can run on anything, including the moon."

Paul Feliciano rode Secretariat in his first two races, but after that, Canadian jockey Ron Turcotte became his regular pilot. A native of Grand Forks, New Brunswick, Ron Turcotte, son of a lumberjack, rode his first race in 1961 as an apprentice jockey, became Canada's leading rider one short year later, and invaded the United States in 1962. Since then his mounts have won more than a million dollars annually. In 1973, Ron's share of the purses was $278,000.

The small, rock-hard, 112 pounder with the ready smile makes few excuses when he loses and takes little of the credit when he wins. "The horse does the running," says Ron Turcotte. "The biggest mistake a rider can make is to feel that he is more important than his horse. . . ."

He is the third and only living jockey to have won two Kentucky Derbys back to back—with Riva Ridge in 1972 and Secretariat in 1973. Two black jockeys did this ahead of him: Isaac Murphy in 1890 and 1891, and Jimmy Winkfield in 1901 and 1902.

In the spring of 1972 Riva Ridge was making all the headlines. He won the Derby and the Belmont and, according to Penny Tweedy, saved the Meadow Stable. "He was my first good one when I took over the operation. . . . He came along after a time of losses, when both my brother and sister were questioning whether we should continue in racing."

By the end of that year, Secretariat, not Riva Ridge, was given top billing. In a short six months the colt, who had only learned to run that June, won $456,404. He was named two-year-old champion and was the first two-year-old ever to be named Horse of the Year.

With Secretariat and Riva Ridge in the barn, Meadow Stable should have been on easy street, but it was not. Mr. Chenery died in January 1973, and inheritance taxes loomed on the horizon. The Meadow Stud was appraised for tax purposes, and Secretariat and Riva Ridge were the greatest assets. Uncle Sam wanted millions, and, of course, in cash. The money had to be raised, and Secretariat and Riva Ridge came to the rescue.

With the assistance of young Seth Hancock, son of the recently deceased Bull Hancock of Claiborne Farm, Mrs. Tweedy arranged to syndicate her two champions for breeding. The proposed syndicated price for Secretariat, the two-year-old champion who had not yet shown his worth as a three year old, was to be $190,000 per share, or a total of $6,080,000; Riva Ridge's price tag was a cool $5,120,000.

In an industry where the record syndication price had been $5,400,000 for Nijinsky, the European champion, experts wondered whether the fees were not too steep. Drawing on foreign as well as American buyers, Seth Hancock completed the deal speedily and with apparent ease. Since then, $500,000

The first two year old ever to be named Horse of the Year, Secretariat celebrated a landmark birthday with trainer Lucien Laurin.

has been offered for a single share of Secretariat and $100,000 is reported to be the going rate for one service.

Horse owners are used to gambling "big," but for that kind of money they wanted a guarantee that the two horses would become good sires. As horses in training cannot be bred or tested, Lloyds of London, the famous underwriters, were called in to insure the two horses' reproductive ability. A policy, with a premium rumored to have cost $500,000, was devised, and both horses were to continue racing under the blue and white Meadow Stable colors until November. With the money almost in the bank, Mrs. Tweedy and the other members of the Meadow family could now enjoy Secretariat's three-year-old year and Riva's fourth and handicap season.

In the spring of 1973, Lucien Laurin's Barn Five at Belmont once again housed Riva Ridge and Secretariat, but that year Secretariat, not Riva, was the superstar. The racing public had made him their hero; everyone wanted to see him run and win, and win he did. The Bay Shore in March at Aqueduct came first and then the Gotham in April. They were easy victories, but a short two weeks before the Kentucky Derby came the Wood Memorial and disaster. Angle Light, owned by Edwin Whittaker and also trained by Lucien Laurin, beat our hero. The racing fraternity was aghast and Lucien Laurin was horrified. Why was their idol beaten? The excuses were many, but perhaps the truth was that the big colt just had not been drilled hard and fast enough before the race. He wasn't on his toes, and Turcotte complained that he could not get Secretariat to take hold of the bit.

The syndicate members began to wonder about their $6,080,000 investment, turf writers added to the gloom, but the racing public kept the faith and made him their 3–2 favorite for the Kentucky Derby.

On Derby Day, 134,476 fans—the biggest crowd ever to attend a race in the United States—descended upon Churchill Downs and bet $7,627,965. Thousands swarmed over the infield and turned Derby Day into a happening. They danced and sang and drank mint juleps out of paper cups; in the boxes, the same drink was being served in silver-plated goblets.

Nineteen million people, all over the country, watched the excitement on TV, and only the big chestnut colt was calm. Secretariat stretched out in his stall and took a forty-five minute nap before the race. Refreshed by his beauty sleep, he walked onto the track like a king. The band struck up "My Old Kentucky Home," and, unencumbered by a lead pony, Secretariat jogged and then cantered toward the starting gate.

Sham was the horse to beat, and beat him he did, although early in the race Secretariat dropped back almost to last, nearly giving his supporters heart failure. Instead of having to worry, they saw the greatest race in the ninety-nine-year history of the Derby. Secretariat set a new record for the mile and one-quarter of 1:59⅖, ending with a blazing 0:23⅕ burst in the final quarter.

This performance stilled his critics, and no one was surprised when two weeks later he mopped up the Preakness. Secretariat broke with the field, and then swooped past his competition. He led for the last three-quarters of a mile and again won by two and one-half lengths over his arch rival, Sham.

He may have broken another record. The automatic timer at Pimlico possibly malfunctioned and the official time of 1:54⅖ for the mile and three-sixteenths has been disputed as being too slow.

With his overwhelming victories in the Derby and Preakness, Secretariat was only a mile and a half away from immortality. Winning the Belmont Stakes would make him the first Triple Crown winner in twenty-five years. After Sir Barton in 1919, only seven other horses had crossed the finish line first in all three grueling races. *Time*, *Newsweek*, *Sports Illustrated* and *The National Observer* took a calculated risk, and ran "Super Red" as their cover story that week.

The tension around Barn Five was electric. Pinkerton guards protected Secretariat, but his human family was more exposed to the public. While Mrs. Tweedy and Laurin fielded the press, Secretariat, ridden by his exercise boy Charley Davis, enjoyed his morning workouts. Later, he cleaned up his ample rations and snoozed in his stall under the watchful eyes of Eddie Sweat, Laurin's top groom for eighteen years.

Secretariat relaxed while Mrs. Tweedy and a staff of secretaries attended to the big horse's fan mail. Forty to a hundred letters arrived daily and every one of them was answered. "It's like taking care of a movie star who can't do anything for himself," said Penny Tweedy.

The greatest pressure was on Laurin. "Sometimes I feel I'm seventy instead of sixty years old," he said, but in his more relaxed moments he exulted in his charge. "This colt is fantastic. . . . I've never seen anything like him and I've been training horses for thirty-three years."

Millions of Americans watched the Belmont on TV, but 67,605 fans crowded into Belmont Park to cheer their superhorse. On the grueling one-and-a-half-mile course, Secretariat proved that he was not just the Horse of the Year, he was the Horse for All Years, in a class with Man o'War and the great Citation.

The hero worship for Secretariat spilled over onto his blonde mistress. On Belmont day, walking to her box, Penny Tweedy was cheered by an entire grandstand. From the two-dollar bettor to the boxholder, all had made Secretariat their king. Through him, she had become their queen.

As post time approached, the crowd quieted down. All eyes were on starter George Cassidy. "They're off," boomed the loudspeaker, and five horses, as if simultaneously stung by a giant hornet, flew out of the starting gate. Secretariat opened a twenty-length lead. Fantastic as this was, the big colt changed gears once more and crossed the finish line in a record 2:24 for the mile and one-half. An unbelievable thirty-one lengths ahead of Twice a Prince, his closest rival, Secretariat could truly be compared to the immortal Eclipse who, in the 1760s, caused the English to say, "Eclipse first—the rest nowhere."

It was only June and the Meadow Stable could race Secretariat until November. "Quit while you are ahead" was the unsolicited advice given Penny Tweedy. "If you want to continue racing him, go to Europe and run him in France, in the Arc de Triomphe. Don't take a chance of getting him beaten here," but Mrs. Tweedy took the risk. "The people love him," she said. "They should have a chance to see him."

After the Belmont, Secretariat had a three-week rest and then flew to Arlington Park, Chicago, to show Middle Westerners his heels in the Arlington Invitational. He won easily by nine lengths, and winged back to spend the month of August with the other socialites in Saratoga.

On August 4, in front of the largest crowd in the history of Saratoga (30,119), Secretariat met older horses for the first time and was beaten by one length in the Whitney Stakes by a horse with the unlikely name of Onion. No one could understand it. The citizens of the famous old spa had decorated Union Avenue with bunting in Meadow Stable's blue and white colors. The upset left them crushed. The betting public took their licking in silence. Lucien Laurin was nonplused, but the answer came twenty-four hours later when Secretariat ran a temperature and came down with a virus infection. The colt could not have felt well on the day of the Whitney. Maybe he tried to tell Eddie Sweat, his groom, but even a horse as smart as Secretariat has a hard time convincing his owner, trainer, and jockey that he would rather stay in bed.

About a month later, he more than redeemed himself in the one-and-one-eighth-mile Marlboro Cup at Belmont in world record time of 1:45⅖. Running against the best older horses, he beat his stablemate Riva Ridge by three and a half lengths, with Cougar II coming in third.

Then came the Woodward, another race starting with the unlucky letter W. Secretariat had been beaten in the Wood and the Whitney; he fared no better in the Woodward. Prove Out, who had been sold by the King Ranch to Hobeau Farm six weeks earlier, bested him by four and a half lengths. It was the worst defeat of his career. The easy explanation was that the champ was tired, but no one really knew.

With only one month to go to his retirement, Secretariat switched to running on grass and ended his career with two smashing victories. In the mile and a half Man o'War Stakes at Belmont, he clipped three fifths of a second off the course mark and romped home in 2:24⅘.

His final race was the Canadian International at Woodbine,

Toronto, on a dreary raw October day. But Secretariat's brilliant performance dispelled the gloom. He warmed the hearts of not only his Meadow Stable family, but of all racing fans, when he ran home in a blaze of glory. With Eddie Maple in the saddle, instead of Ron Turcotte who had drawn a five-day suspension, Super Red covered the mile and five-eighths in a sizzling 2:41⅘, beating Big Spruce, his nearest rival, by six and a half lengths.

Now all was over but the shouting. On Election Day, Secretariat made a farewell appearance at the Big A, whose gate receipts and pari-mutuel handle had swelled every time his name appeared on the program.

With Ron Turcotte in the saddle, the big colt said goodbye to his fans. His chestnut coat gleamed, and he looked as beautiful as ever as he posed for the seventeenth and last time in the winner's circle. "He doesn't know why he's here," said Penny Tweedy. "He has not run, he's not tired, and he has not won."

Mrs. Tweedy received a bouquet of roses and Eddie Sweat, Secretariat's groom, and Charley Davis, his exercise boy, each received a wrist watch from a grateful New York Racing Association.

RACING RECORD

Year	Age	Starts	1st	2nd	3rd	Earnings
1972	2	9	7	1	0	$ 456,404
1973	3	12	9	2	1	860,404
	Totals	21	16	3	1	$1,316,808

Secretariat had raced twenty-one times, won sixteen, been beaten four times, and disqualified once. He broke five track and two world records and earned $860,404 in 1973; more money in a single year than any horse before him. His total bank account of $1,316,808 ranked him as the fourth greatest money winner of all time. Only Kelso, Round Table, and Buckpasser had earned more than he.

With the field some thirty lengths behind him, Ron Turcotte had trouble locating Secretariat's lagging competition.

While Secretariat was being let down and readied for his trip to Kentucky to meet his harem at Claiborne, the public and the press continued to talk and write about him. They called him The Great Horse of this generation and compared him to Man o'War. Both were handsome chestnuts who started twenty-one times. Man o'War scored twenty victories, four more than Secretariat, but Super Red, due to the tremendous increase in the size of the purses, amassed five times as much money as Big Red.

Both horses finished their racing careers at the age of three in Canada, and were then sent to stud in Kentucky.

Man o'War was bred to an undistinguished group of mares, poor runners and poor producers, belonging to Mr. Riddle and his friends. Despite the mediocre quality of the dams, among the first ninety foals were twenty-six stakes winners—a fantastic record.

Secretariat will be bred to the finest broodmares, but even so, only time will tell whether his performance at stud will match his superb record on the track.

Mrs. Tweedy and The Meadow family had one more big day while Secretariat was settling in at Claiborne. The Eclipse Awards dinner, for top honors in 1973 thoroughbred racing, was held in Bal Harbour, Florida, on January 11, 1974. Once again Secretariat won it all: Horse of the Year for the second successive season, the best three-year-old colt, and, for his superb performances on turf in both the Man o'War and the Canadian International, the Best Grass Horse of 1973.

Secretariat has firmly established his place as one of the all-time greats. Some will say that he was better than Man o'War and the fantastic Citation, others will disagree. But no

Ambling down Belmont's victory lane, Secretariat was flanked by proud mistress, Helen "Penny" Tweedy (right) and Elizabeth Ham.

one will dispute that, thanks to color TV, this beautiful chestnut horse and the ebullient Penny Tweedy gave millions of Americans the opportunity to share in the thrill and excitement of thoroughbred racing. Seated comfortably in their living rooms, all America witnessed true equine nobility, not soon—if ever—to be seen again.

So far, the seventies have produced Canonero II, Riva Ridge, Little Current—who, in 1971, 1972 and 1974, won two out of three legs of the Triple Crown—and Secretariat, who swept all before him in 1973. Perhaps the gods will continue to smile and not make the racing public wait another twenty-five years for the coronation of the tenth Triple Crown winner!

<table>
<tr><td rowspan="4">SIR BARTON
(1916–1937)</td><td rowspan="2">*STAR SHOOT, 1898</td><td>Isinglass</td></tr>
<tr><td>Astrology</td></tr>
<tr><td rowspan="2">LADY STERLING, 1899</td><td>Hanover</td></tr>
<tr><td>*Aquila</td></tr>
</table>

3
Sir Barton
The First Triple Crown Winner

It all started with Sir Barton, who was sired by an English horse, was owned by a Canadian, and won America's first Triple Crown even before it officially existed. The great Man o'War's senior by one year, Sir Barton was a bad-tempered but good-looking chestnut colt by *Star Shoot out of Lady Sterling. He was foaled in 1916 at John E. Madden's Hamburg Place in Lexington, Kentucky.

Although John Madden considered August Belmont, who bred Man o'War, the greatest breeder in America, the compliment could well have been reciprocated. Hamburg Place was a virtual assembly line of good horses, turning out as many as 150 yearlings and horses-in-training each year. "The Wizard of Hamburg Place" bred three of America's great horses: Old Rosebud, Sir Barton, and Grey Lag. Five Kentucky Derby winners were foaled at his farm, and for eleven years he was top breeder in the United States.

In 1914, *Star Shoot, Sir Barton's sire, was the most successful stallion in the United States and occupied Box One at Hamburg Place. *Star Shoot had raced ten times in England, but he became "winded"—had difficulty breathing

—and was retired to stud. Although his sire, Isinglass, had won the English Derby and his dam, Astrology, was sired by another English Derby winner, Hermit, *Star Shoot turned out to be a "stall-flower" and few fillies came to call.

In 1901 he was sold to Catesby Woodford of Paris, Kentucky. Crossing the Atlantic improved his love life and, as his colts and fillies started to appear in the winner's circle of tracks all over the United States, the name *Star Shoot became famous. In 1912 he was bought by John E. Madden to head the stallion roster at Hamburg Place and, although *Star Shoot became blind, he continued as a stallion until his death in 1919, aged twenty-one and the sire of 2,356 winners!

In 1915, Madden bred *Star Shoot to Lady Sterling. This was truly a senior citizen nuptial: he was seventeen, and his blushing bride a well-preserved sixteen. That winter, the English trainer, Vivian Gooch, visited Hamburg Place and Madden gave his good friend a one-half interest in the unborn colt who became Sir Barton.

The foal was born April 26, 1916, in the stable which was also the nursery of four other Kentucky Derby winners: Old Rosebud, Paul Jones, Zev, and Flying Ebony.

While Sir Barton was still a weanling, Madden was so impressed with the colt that he purchased back the half-interest he had given Vivian Gooch. In 1918, his two-year-old year, Sir Barton started to race, wearing the cherry and white colors of John E. Madden.

The small chestnut colt was brought along slowly by Madden, who believed that a two year old was just a baby, and that great harm could be done to the developing youngster by hard early racing. Today, in our inflated economy, keeping a race horse has become so expensive that owners are tempted to race their horses too much, too soon, and too young. In 1918, a conscientious owner could afford to take his time.

Sir Barton's early races were primarily for experience. He raced six times and placed only once, yet the experts took notice of him. He was a likely colt of good conformation and breeding and, on paper, he had all the qualifications necessary for an excellent race horse. Sir Barton's potential was apparent to Commander John Kenneth Leveson Ross, a Canadian friend of Madden's, and to Ross's trainer, Harvey Guy Bedwell. As Madden was primarily a breeder, he agreed to sell Sir Barton to Ross for $10,000—a good price for a two year old in 1918.

The Canadian's orange and black silks had first appeared at Bowie, in Maryland, in 1915, and by 1918 Ross was ready to build the best stable in America. To accomplish this, he engaged Harvey Guy Bedwell, who, for six consecutive years, had saddled more winners than any other trainer in America. Bedwell had achieved his success with cheap horses; working for Ross, he would have a chance to race the best.

Commander Ross was a gentleman of the old school. Tall and athletic, he had been a college football player, but his two loves were the sea and horses. His great wealth, inherited from his father, one of the founders of the Canadian Pacific Railroad, made it possible for him to indulge both his hobbies. An ardent yachtsman, he was invited to join the Royal Yacht Squadron at Cowes, England, an honor on a par with becoming a member of The Jockey Club.

Ross spent money in the grand manner, both for horses and for wagering. In the heyday of bookmakers, "S.P." meant "Starting Price," the odds quoted at post time of each race. Ross sent a telegram to his bookmaker—highly illegal, of course—betting "Twenty thousand S. P. my entry second race tomorrow," meaning a bet of $20,000 to win. The bookie understood this to mean $20,000 straight, to win, and another $20,000 to place; or a bet twice as large as intended.

Luckily, the horse won for a total of $160,000, of which the place bet of $20,000 at 2 to 1 represented $40,000. Ross refused to take the place money and told his agent "Give it back to the bookmakers."

Ross was always a good sportsman. Once, after a judge's bad decision took away a victory from a Ross horse, the commander said to his son, "Jim, in racing, . . . the decision of the judges must always be accepted as final. You must always remember that . . . without the uncertainty of who is going to win, the sport couldn't survive. It's what we call the glorious uncertainty of racing!"

Sir Barton's trainer was as reserved as Ross was friendly and outgoing. Harvey Guy "Hard Guy" Bedwell was a hard-hitting, relentless pro whose only interest was winning horse races. A taciturn westerner, lean and mean, he rarely smiled and under pressure became an irascible gum and cigar chewing automaton.

Bedwell was a thorough horseman. A member of a California gold rush family, he became an Oregon cowboy and worked cattle on the plains with Sam Hildreth and Tom Smith, both of whom also later became leading race-horse trainers. This day-to-day experience with range animals was to give the three trainers the ability to keep that most fragile creature, the race horse, sound enough to race and to win.

Bedwell drifted from cowpunching to running a livery stable in Grand Junction, Colorado, and then to racing at the local fairgrounds. As an owner-trainer, he was most successful on the western circuit, but the purses were small and Bedwell decided to head east where the big money lay.

At the age of 34 he made his move and became an immediate success. In his first season at the Empire City race track in New York, he saddled sixteen winners in fourteen days. The boy from the West had arrived.

Bedwell had many theories about conditioning. One was to keep his horses standing with their feet in pails of mud; this, he believed, kept the hoof walls from drying out and becoming brittle. Every night, except the one before a race, each horse received a cooked feed of grain, supplemented by Bedwell's own mixture of four kinds of hay. "A good hay-eater is a good race horse," he pronounced.

"Hard Guy" Bedwell took excellent care of his horses, but he was hard on his men and on himself. He knew that watching over race horses was not an eight-hour-a-day occupation, and he expected his grooms to work all hours until the job was done. When Sir Barton developed a severe case of blood poisoning and almost died, Bedwell himself nursed the colt, never leaving his side until the crisis was past.

Like all good trainers, Bedwell was a horse psychologist, and Sir Barton proved to be his most puzzling patient. The colt disliked everybody, from the human beings around him to the stable dogs and cats whom he would kick and bite. Perhaps the colt was too sick to savage his trainer, or perhaps he knew when he had met his match, but he never tried any of his tricks with Bedwell.

Typically, after the colt had recovered, Bedwell refused to take credit for the recovery, claiming that Sir Barton's inherent good health and courage had pulled him through.

Perhaps one reason for Sir Barton's ill temper was his feet. Like many of *Star Shoot's get, he had shelly hooves with weak walls that would not hold the horseshoe nails. His feet were always tender and, in later years, to cushion the hoof and ease the pain, the Ross blacksmith placed pads of piano felt between the hoof and the shoe. This helped Sir Barton's aching feet, but it also made losing his carefully handmade shoes that much easier. Sir Barton threw his shoes like confetti, and in one early race lost all four, still crossing the finish line in second place. After the last race that day, the trainer sent out a harrow to drag the track and recover the shoes.

Bedwell enjoyed a sharp horse-trade. During World War I, there was a serious question as to whether oats would be rationed. If they were, a non-essential animal like the race horse would be at the bottom of the list. At this uncertain moment, Bedwell persuaded a jittery trainer, "Pop" Schorr, to sell him a good horse named Cudgel. Schorr was cutting down his string in anticipation of rationing.

The next day there was an official press release that grain would not be controlled, and Schorr was distraught. He begged Bedwell to take back the money, with a thousand dollar bonus, but Bedwell refused. Schorr did everything to change Bedwell's mind, including telling Bedwell that Mrs. Schorr would never forgive him when she heard about the deal.

When Bedwell met Mrs. Schorr that same day, he said, "Mom, Pop's scared you're going to kill him because I bought that horse."

Mom replied, "Listen, Mr. Guy Bedwell, twenty-five thousand dollars can never break its leg. A horse can."

Bedwell's home was a 106-acre farm near Laurel, Maryland,

called Yarrow Brae. Next to it was Bolingbrook, a much larger estate which Ross bought. Combined with Yarrow Brae, this acreage became the home base and stud farm of the Ross stable.

The year 1918 was a big one for the Ross stable. After Hard Guy Bedwell's first year with Ross, the commander's horses led the annual list of winning owners. It may not sound impressive by today's standards, but the thirty-two horses carrying the orange and black silks of Commander John Kenneth Leveson Ross won $99,179.

Sir Barton's contribution was small—a mere $4,113. Ross had bought the colt in the middle of his two-year-old year, and the Hopeful at Saratoga in August was Sir Barton's first race wearing the Ross colors. For the commander and Bedwell, the race would better have been named the Hopeless. Their colt came in a poor fifteenth behind Eternal.

The Futurity, one month later at Belmont, was a different story. Sir Barton, responding to Bedwell's training methods, began to look and act like a race horse. Ridden in this race by the great jockey, Earl Sande, Sir Barton lunged to the post, his small, chestnut body gleaming, his ears pricked, and his expression alert and ready for business. He was just as ill-tempered and ornery, but he was starting to show that he wanted to run and win.

The colt was still green and, even with Sande in the saddle, they were left in a tangle at the start and hemmed in by the pack. It wasn't until the last furlong that Sande managed to find an opening and Sir Barton gave the winner, Dunboyne, a run for the money. Dunboyne won, but Sir Barton was a good second. Thus ended 1918 for Sir Barton, with one second in six starts.

The Ross stable again dominated American racing in 1919, but this time Sir Barton would contribute his share. At the beginning of the season, Billy Kelly, his stablemate—not Sir Barton—was its star. Billy Kelly was no beauty; he was a small, skinny gelding who looked more like a polo pony than a race horse. But when he ran, the ugly duckling turned into a beautiful swan.

Early in May, Billy Kelly and Sir Barton were shipped from the farm in Maryland to Churchill Downs for the Kentucky Derby. They traveled like royalty, in a special car attached to the Baltimore-Louisville Express. Accompanying them were the assistant trainer, the blacksmith, and an assortment of grooms, watchmen, watchdogs, stable pets, and lead ponies. Feed and bedding for their entire stay filled another car, and even their drinking water was brought from Maryland. Bedwell was taking no chances.

Earl Sande, regular jockey for the Ross stable, thought that Billy Kelly had the best chance to win the Derby and chose him for his mount. Johnny Loftus, who had won the 1916 Kentucky Derby, was chosen as Sir Barton's pilot. A cool rider, credited with having the proverbial ice water in his veins, Loftus was the very picture of a modern, lean, and hungry jockey, continually starving himself to make the weight.

Eternal, owned by John McClelland, was picked to win, with Billy Kelly as the second favorite. In the eyes of the public, Sir Barton, still a maiden, was along for the ride. Because Sir Barton had not yet won a race, he was given a twelve-pound maiden-allowance, and Billy Kelly received a three-pound gelding-allowance. (As experts feel that one pound of weight is equal to one length at the finish, the Ross horses were at a considerable advantage.)

Bedwell was high on Sir Barton and thought him better than Billy Kelly. In a private trial, Sir Barton had outrun Billy Kelly, but nobody knew this except Bedwell, Ross, the exercise boy, and a clocker who was paid to keep silent.

Derby Day at Churchill Downs came with a wet, heavy track. The famous twin spires were shrouded in mist, and the hundreds of blooms so patiently manicured to look their best were wet and soggy. Sir Barton, with his often sore feet, was a good mudder and loved the sloppy going. He bucked and played going to the post. For once the track would not sting his feet. By contrast, Eternal, the favorite, liked a hard track.

Earl Sande was told to hold Billy Kelly off the pace until the stretch and then to make his move. Johnny Loftus, Sir Barton's jockey, was ordered to go to the front and try to stay there. As Loftus said, "I got around the last turn in front, stood in my stirrups, but failed to see Sande and Billy Kelly. I thought, What a shame. . . . Seeing nothing of Billy Kelly I gave him (Sir Barton) a cut with the whip and he jumped off as if it were the start. Then I rode him the rest of the way, figuring to hell with Bedwell, Sande and Billy Kelly, and won by open daylight. Billy Kelly . . . got up to be second." Eternal came in last.

Two records were set that day: for the first time, a horse broke his maiden by winning the Derby and, as another first, stablemates Sir Barton and Billy Kelly finished one–two. But Commander Ross missed the great moment. The day before the race, his father-in-law suffered a severe stroke and the Rosses had returned to Toronto.

It was a clear-cut victory, but the handicappers were still not convinced. Billy Kelly and Eternal had given Sir Barton seven and ten pounds respectively in the Derby. The Preakness, at equal weights four days later, would tell the true story.

The Preakness, at Pimlico, was to be the decisive battle between Eternal and Sir Barton. Eternal's followers felt that the muddy Derby track had caused his defeat, but the Preakness track would be hard and fast. Twelve horses were entered, as in the Derby, and although the attendance was smaller, the purse was $5,000 larger.

As in the Derby, Loftus was told to go as fast as he could right from the start. He went to the lead while rounding the turn into the backstretch, set a terrific pace, and won by four lengths, eased up. Harvey Guy Bedwell had turned Sir Barton into a first-class racing machine! Eternal was second, but driving at the finish.

Ten days later Sir Barton was entered in the one-mile Withers at Belmont Park, New York, and a favorite to win over his old rival Eternal. Bedwell's instructions to Loftus were different this time. Noticing that Eternal tended to drift toward the center of the track on the last turn, he told Loftus to stay behind Eternal until the head of the stretch. Eternal drifted out as predicted, Loftus shot Sir Barton between Eternal and the rail, and won by two and one-half lengths, eased up.

By now there was no question that Sir Barton was a superhorse. Everyone awaited the Belmont Stakes two and one-half weeks later—then, as now, the most severe test of three year olds. This classic, at even weights, so discouraged the competition that there were only two other entries, Sweep On and Natural Bridge, both owned by the Long Island business magnate, W. R. Coe. As the three horses paraded around Belmont's tree-shaded paddock, everyone realized that the race would be no contest.

Natural Bridge tried valiantly to set the pace, but floundered in the stretch as did his stablemate, Sweep On. Sir Barton again won eased up and set a new American record of 2:17$\frac{2}{5}$ for the mile and three-eighths.

In twenty-two days Sir Barton had won the three races of what was to become the Triple Crown—and also mopped up the Withers. In the next fifty-four years, only eight other horses would win the Triple Crown, and Count Fleet alone, in 1943, would again make a clean sweep of the four races.

Much later, John McClelland, the owner of Eternal, said of Sir Barton, "That's the best three-year-old I've seen in my thirty years on the turf, and I've seen some great horses."

Sir Barton was at his zenith, and, looking back, perhaps Ross should have quit at the top. Bedwell, great trainer that he was, made a serious mistake in judgment; he entered Sir Barton in the Dwyer. There was simply not time enough in the two weeks following the Belmont for Sir Barton to snap back from the exertions of the twenty-two days before. He was just too tired; and he lost to Purchase, an extraordinarily good-looking grandson of Ormonde, the English Triple Crown winner.

Sir Barton ended his season with a bang, however, winning two weight-for-age races at Pimlico. He had finished his three-year-old year having raced thirteen times, with eight wins—including the Triple Crown, three seconds, and two thirds. He was never out of the money and brought home $88,250.

Once again, in 1919, the Ross stable was the leading money winner with $209,303. This was a fantastic record in the days when the average price of a yearling at the Saratoga sales was slightly over $1,000. Man o'War was the sixth highest-priced horse of the 1918 sale at $5,000.

1919 was Sir Barton's Triple Crown year but, by 1920, Man o'War, a giant of a horse, dominated American racing. Millions came to know him as "Big Red" and his performances dwarfed the competition. He broke every record and was said to have broken the heart of many of his adversaries.

In two years of racing, Man o'War had won twenty out of twenty-one races. Poor judgment on the part of his jockey, not poor performance, was the cause of his only defeat.

Man o'War would almost certainly have won the Triple Crown, had he been entered in all three contests. Samuel Riddle, his owner, felt that long races like the Kentucky Derby and the Preakness were too close together and too exhausting so early in the racing season. He did not enter Man o'War in the Derby.

The year 1920 seemed destined to see a confrontation between the three-year-old Man o'War and the four-year-old Sir Barton. Certainly, nothing is better for gate receipts than a match race between two giants. Promoters like this sort of fight to the finish between champions, but most horsemen do not. Commander Ross was of the latter opinion. "Match races are wonderful in prospect . . . that's why they're run . . . but, as good racing goes, they are often terrible duds."

The pressure for the race was enormous. Matt Winn wanted it held at Churchill Downs; the management of Laurel Race Track put in their bid; but Sam Riddle, Man o'War's owner, and Commander Ross decided to accept the invitation of Kenilworth Park near Windsor, Ontario. The date set was October 12th, 1920, and the race—at one and one-quarter miles—was for $75,000, plus a $5,000 gold cup. Although Commander Ross did not feel that Sir Barton could beat the great Man o'War, he thought he could give him a run for his money. And, being a staunch Canadian, he was happy to have this important meeting on Canadian soil.

For Sir Barton and the Ross stable, the race was ill-fated. Hard Guy Bedwell liked nothing about Kenilworth. He knew his horse was not in top form and that the hard surface of the track would bother Sir Barton's tender feet. He would rather have withdrawn the colt, but good sportsmanship did not permit it.

An ill-tempered and ornery colt, Sir Barton had tender feet that required carefully handmade shoes.

The tension caught up with everyone. Bedwell lost weight like Sir Barton lost shoes, and by the day of the race he looked like a cigar-chewing ghost. Earl Sande suffered a severe case of nerves, and Bedwell and Ross, fearing that the pressure was just too much for their contract jockey, took him off the horse and substituted Frank Keogh as the rider. Although Sande continued to work for the Ross stable, he never forgave Bedwell.

The crowds that afternoon at Kenilworth Park were larger than they had ever been or would be again. Thousands came to see "the race of the century," from small time bettors to racing greats like Foxhall Keene, Joseph Widener, Walter Jeffords, and William Woodward.

The racegoers made Man o'War the overwhelming favorite and they were right. Sir Barton broke well at the start and took the lead for a few hundred yards. For a brief moment, it looked as if it might be a race worthy of the two great horses, but when they passed the judges' stand for the first time, Frank Keogh was already using the whip. Effortlessly, Man o'War extended his flawless gallop, and Sir Barton, his tender feet jarred by every stride, courageously struggled on. It was no contest: Man o'War beat him easily by seven lengths, covering the one and one-quarter miles in 2:03, a new track record.

The Kenilworth Gold Cup was Man o'War's last race. Although he was only a three year old, Mr. Riddle, his owner, was much more eager to begin Man o'War's career at stud than to win more races. It was almost the same for Sir Barton, who raced three more times without winning and was then retired to stud. Perhaps his heart was another that Man o'War had broken.

RACING RECORD

Year	Age	Starts	1st	2nd	3rd	Earnings
1918	2	6	0	1	0	$ 4,113
1919	3	13	8	3	2	88,250
1920	4	12	5	2	3	24,494
	Totals	31	13	6	5	$116,857

Both Commander John Kenneth Leveson Ross and Sir Barton's racing careers were meteoric. Sir Barton had his great Triple Crown year in 1919, and the Ross stable was the leading money winner in the United States for 1918 and 1919.

In 1922, Ross sold his Triple Crown winner to the Audley Farm in Virginia, where Sir Barton stood at stud until 1933. In 1927, financial reverses caused Ross to give up racing entirely, and he retired to live out his life in Jamaica, in the West Indies. He died in 1951 and, by his express wish, was reunited with his other great love by being buried at sea.

Sir Barton's career at stud was to prove far from spectacular. He sired a few winners, but none was outstanding. He ended his days on the United States Remount ranch, the government horse-breeding farm at Douglas, Wyoming, where he died in 1937, aged twenty-one.

His name is little known today, but in the last fifty-six years there have been only nine winners of the Triple Crown, and he was the first. As John Madden, Sir Barton's breeder, said, "Opinions die, records live."

GALLANT FOX (1927–1954)	**SIR GALLAHAD III, 1920*	**Teddy*	
		Plucky Liege	
	MARGUERITE, 1920	*Celt*	
		**Fairy Ray*	

4
Gallant Fox & Omaha

The Fox of Belair and His Greatest Son

IN FIFTY-FIVE YEARS, only once has a father been succeeded by his son as the wearer of the Triple Crown: Belair Stud's Gallant Fox in 1930 and his son, Omaha, in 1935. Both horses were trained by the great "Sunny Jim" Fitzsimmons and were owned by William Woodward, Sr.—banker, and president of The Jockey Club.

In those years America was in the depths of the Great Depression and only the fewest of the few—the very rich—owned race horses. The stock market crash of 1929 reached many, but Mr. Woodward was not among them, and Gallant Fox and Omaha went first class all the way. Each was born with a silver bit in his mouth.

They were foaled at Claiborne Farm near Lexington, Kentucky, then as now the greatest thoroughbred nursery in the land. From there, they were sent to the manicured pastures of Belair, Mr. Woodward's palatial 3,000-acre Maryland estate, and as two year olds they were destined for "Sunny Jim's" barn at the track.

William Woodward, Sr., their owner, was a patrician. A man of distinguished appearance and impeccable breeding, he was charming, worldly, and a little pompous. After graduating from Harvard Law School in 1903, he went into banking and succeeded his uncle as president of the Hanover National Bank.

In later years Woodward often told a story about himself as a young bank officer. "I smoked a great many cigarettes in those days," he recalled. "One morning one of my superiors suggested that a banker should smoke cigars.

"It was not so hard to learn banking," Woodward remembered, "but those cigars made me deathly sick."

William Woodward had first become interested in racing while with the American Embassy in London. Later he maintained a stable at the true birthplace of thoroughbred racing, Newmarket, and his trainer was Captain Cecil Boyd-Rochfort, who also trained for the royal family.

In 1910, Woodward inherited Belair Stud near Bowie, Maryland. Founded by Governor Samuel Ogle in the eighteenth century, Belair had been a stud farm for two hundred years. In the nineteenth century another governor of Maryland, Oden Bowie (after whom Bowie Race Track was named), acquired a portion of the stud. Its peak was reached, however, under William Woodward, with such horses as Gallant Fox, Omaha, Granville, and Nashua.

The entrance to Belair was through an avenue of magnificent old oaks. The formal Georgian mansion was filled with Sheraton and Hepplewhite furniture, Georgian silver, and a collection of sporting paintings now housed in the Baltimore Museum of Fine Arts.

"I loved to visit Belair," recalls a friend of the Woodwards' daughter, Edith. "Your soiled laundry was whisked away almost before you undressed," she remembers. "A butler and scads of footmen and maids ran the house, and we ate off Crown Derby china. Mrs. Woodward worried that some might be broken, but Mr. Woodward loved beautiful things and wanted them used."

On Sunday mornings the yearlings were always inspected. Usually a large house-party was in residence, but even if only one of the many daughters and a friend were there, the ceremony was just the same. A groom brought out each colt, paraded it in front of the guests, and then returned it to its stall. At the end of the ceremony Mr. Woodward would ask each girl to give him a critique of the horses she had seen. "We were scared to death of him," Edith's friend recalled, "but we adored the grown-up way he treated us."

William Woodward was elected to The Jockey Club, the governing body of American racing, in 1917. He maintained a stable for many years, but it was not until 1923, when Edward James "Sunny Jim" Fitzsimmons became his trainer, that Belair's red and white polka dots, which Woodward had purchased from the estate of England's Earl of Zetland, hit the big time.

Fitzsimmons, born in 1874, was the son of Irish immigrant parents. His father was a huckster in Brooklyn, and at the age of ten, young Fitzsimmons went to work. His first job was in the kitchen of the nearby Sheepshead Bay race track. Later he was promoted to galloping horses.

Sunny Jim became a jockey, but not a very good one, and eventually gravitated into training. He saddled his first winner on August 7, 1900. For the next twenty-three years he made an adequate living, but when William Woodward asked him to become Belair's trainer, he had a chance to show what he could do with good horses and lots of them. Later, he also trained for the Wheatley Stables owned by Mrs. Henry Carnegie Phipps and her brother, Ogden Mills. To the end of his life "Mr. Fitz" worked exclusively for Belair and Wheatley, and both stables gained prominence under him.

Fitzsimmons was a master trainer of the old, tough school. His workouts for horses were sharp and frequent, a stern regime which weeded out the weak. With two such wealthy owners, Fitzsimmons could afford to discard all but the very best. He was not infallible, however, and sold the great Seabiscuit to Californian Charles S. Howard. As a two year old, Seabiscuit had won only $12,510. In his three-year-old year he was crossing the finish line first in some minor races. Fitzsimmons had so many (or so he thought) better horses in his barn that, for $7,500, he let Howard have this bay grandson of Man o'War who was to become the world's leading money winner.

In a racing career which spanned seventy-eight years, Mr. Fitz's horses won 2,275 races and $13,082,911. As trainer emeritus, stop watch in hand, the beloved, badly crippled old man was still supervising workouts until his death in 1966 at the ripe old age of ninety-one.

The Woodward-Fitzsimmons double Triple Crown started with *Sir Gallahad III, a French stallion of English lineage going back to St. Simon. *Sir Gallahad was imported for $125,000 by a group of wealthy men headed by A. B. Hancock, Sr. of Claiborne Farm. Their number included Marshall Field, R. A. Fairbairn, and William Woodward. This was one of the first syndications arranged by Hancock, whose grandson, Seth, was to syndicate Secretariat and Riva Ridge for a record $11 million.

*Sir Gallahad III stood at Hancock's Claiborne Stud, near

Lexington, and became one of this country's top sires. In his first year at stud, *Sir Gallahad was bred to Marguerite, a mare by Celt, who was a grandson of Domino. Marguerite had started only once, was injured, and was retired as a broodmare. On March 23, 1927, Gallant Fox, her big bay colt, was foaled at Claiborne Stud.

Hancock and Woodward were close friends and, through the years, Mr. Woodward kept about twenty broodmares at Claiborne. The foals stayed in Kentucky until they were weanlings and then were moved to Belair, where they began to learn about the life of a race horse.

Gallant Fox had everything; he was royally bred, he had the best upbringing money could buy, and when he went to the track, Fitzsimmons, a topnotch teacher, introduced him to racing. Nevertheless, the rangy bay colt with the large white blaze on his face was like a typical rich man's son who did not have to work for his eduation. He enjoyed running and beating other horses, but he was a stargazer, fascinated by everything he saw around him. Above all, he was lazy. These two faults caused him grief in his two-year-old year.

He started his racing career at Aqueduct, and in the Tremont Stakes, his second time out, a low-flying plane so fascinated the colt that he paid no attention to his jockey. He was left at the gate and failed to place for the only time in his entire career.

He lost the Futurity at Belmont through his other bad habit, laziness. According to Mr. Fitz, "So long as he had competition he would run like the wind; when he got ahead he would slow down to a walk." In the Futurity, Gallant Fox had the race won, but after taking the lead, he decided that it was time to coast. Since he was wearing blinkers, he did not see two horses gaining on him until it was too late. He came in third.

To make "The Fox" exert himself during workouts, Fitzsimmons stationed horses at strategic locations around the track. Like a boxer's sparring partner, as soon as Gallant Fox had used up one running mate, another took over to make him extend himself.

Gallant Fox's last two-year-old race was the Junior Champion Stakes at Aqueduct on September 28, 1929. He ran one mile in 1:38, winning by two lengths over Fair Stable's Desert Light. It was a promising ending to a moderate year. He had run a total of seven times, won two, and was out of the money only once.

Gallant Fox was then retired to Belair for the winter. Mr. Woodward believed that a two year old was physically immature and that too much early racing would prevent the horse from developing his full potential. Woodward was wealthy enough to pass up the $60,000 Pimlico Futurity for two year olds and to save his colt for the next year. This decision may have won him the Triple Crown in 1930.

Racing in the 1930s was a gentleman's game; most owners were wealthy sportsmen who raced for glory rather than for purses. It was a hobby, like yachting or owning a shooting plantation in the Carolinas.

Keeping a horse in training then cost a fraction of today's twelve thousand dollars a year, and the Internal Revenue Service was not a factor. Now, race-horse owners must show a profit or be taxed out of existence. Consequently, present-day owners will often over-race a two year old and break him down before his all important three-year-old year. In the thirties, there was no such temptation.

The year 1930 was a big one for William Woodward,

Gallant Fox, his jockey Earl Sande, and Sunny Jim Fitzsimmons. The master of Belair became chairman of The Jockey Club, Gallant Fox won the Triple Crown, Sande earned more than thirty thousand dollars, and Fitzsimmons became the top trainer in the country.

To be chairman of The Jockey Club, that august body which rules racing, is a great honor and a tremendous responsibility. For nineteen years Mr. Woodward remained its head, and under his chairmanship the starting gate and the patrol and finish cameras were first used.

Before the beginning of Gallant Fox's three-year-old year, Woodward and Fitzsimmons decided that The Fox had great potential, but only with a master jockey. The recently retired Earl Sande had been the best, and Mr. Woodward wanted to lure him back into the saddle.

Sande had had a bad fall at Saratoga in 1924 and decided, for the first time, to hang up his tack. This decision lasted only until the next spring when he started looking for a Derby mount. The favorite was Quatrain, and Sande, with the owner's permission, tried to buy the ride from Quatrain's jockey. Sande was not successful and searched around for another mount. He found one, and rode the winner, Flying Ebony.

After that, Sande retired again to a career of training until, in 1930, Mr. Woodward asked him to ride Gallant Fox. Sande agreed and the carrot on the stick was that he was to receive ten percent of the prize money, instead of his usual $1,500 monthly retainer. This was just after the disastrous 1929 stock market crash and Sande, instead of watching his stocks dwindle, banked $30,827.50 as his ten percent of Gallant Fox's Triple Crown year.

A fantastic jockey, Sande rode 3,663 mounts in his lifetime, but more important, he won twenty-six percent of his races and was "in the money" most of the time.

Gallant Fox had grown over the winter. He looked less coltish and seemed ready for serious work. Many experts feel that, in winning a horse race, ninety percent is up to the horse, while the other ten percent is divided between jockey and trainer. Earl Sande and Mr. Fitz were loaded with talent; the colt now had to prove that he was a winner.

Gallant Fox's first three-year-old race was the Wood Memorial at Jamaica in 1930. It was Earl Sande's introduction to the colt, and he immediately established a rapport with his mount in the one-mile-and-seventy-yard race. Sande "rated"—paced—him perfectly, winning by a comfortable four lengths.

The press took notice and started to write about Gallant Fox as a serious candidate for the three big races—the Kentucky Derby, the Preakness, and the Belmont. The colt's manner of winning was reported as "airy" and the odds on his future performances were drastically cut by the bookmakers. That year, the Preakness was held before the Derby, and the Belair Fox went to Pimlico as the favorite for the thirty-ninth running of that historic stakes race.

It was the first time that a starting gate was used in any of the classic races. Until then, a walk-up start was the most popular method, but the experts felt that the electrically operated gate would be fairer, with fewer delays and less chance of injury to the valuable youngsters. Its detractors claimed that the "machine" obstructed the view of the all-important start and that asking a horse to accelerate from a standstill put too much strain on his legs. The advantages outweighed the disadvantages, and since 1930 starting gates have been used at most tracks.

Preakness Day was almost a state holiday in Maryland, and Mr. Woodward hoped that The Fox would do well in the state where he was raised.

Gallant Fox came to that new monster, the starting gate, on his best behavior. He had overcome his coltish curiosity and was all business under Earl Sande. Responding to his jockey's sympathetic handling, The Fox won going away.

The race took surprisingly little out of him. Tired horses often go off their feed, but Gallant Fox polished off his supper and wondered what all the fuss was about. He was not impressed by the quantity of oats that his winnings, $51,925, would buy. Several days later, he was more than ready for the train trip to Louisville and the Kentucky Derby.

Only Triple Crown winner to sire a Triple Crown winner, Gallant Fox also had the distinction of running in the Preakness *before* the Derby in 1930.

Lord Derby, after whose ancestor the English Derby was named, was the guest of honor at Churchill Downs. He saw the race from a special pagoda in the infield. The weather, a slow English-style drizzle, made him feel completely at home.

Gallant Fox and Sande were the overwhelming favorites and won with ease. The Fox broke no records, but Earl Sande tied one. He became the second jockey in the history of the Kentucky Derby to win the race three times. He had ridden Zev in 1923, Flying Ebony in 1925, and now, with Gallant Fox, he equaled the record of Isaac Murphy, the famous black jockey who had three wins between 1884 and 1891.

Lord Derby presented Mr. Woodward with the trophy and graciously said, "I came five thousand miles to watch this Derby. . . . I was pleased to see a good horse win."

Gallant Fox had won his second classic and become a star.

The racing scene moved to New York where Gallant Fox was to race Harry Payne Whitney's Whichone in the Belmont Stakes. The weather was again wet, but a good crowd risked a drenching to see the race. Gallant Fox was a "mudder" and the heavy going never bothered him. The Woodwards and their daughters were in their box. Mrs. Woodward, highly decorative in her picture hat and white gloves (and an umbrella, we hope), smiled at the crowd of well-wishers.

Gallant Fox was feeling his oats, or perhaps all the money he had made in the past few weeks had gone to his head. He was fractious at the start. As the New York tracks were not to install the starting gate until the following year, The Fox caused a false start. Sande brought him back quickly and the race began.

Gallant Fox went to the front and stayed there all the way. Whichone came up from behind to challenge, but "Handy

Sande" just let out a notch and Gallant Fox drew smoothly away to a three-length victory.

The Woodwards were delighted. In 1930, with no radio or TV coverage to publicize their victory, the presentation ceremony was much more restrained. Mr. Woodward went down alone to the winner's circle to receive the trophy; the rest of the family remained in the box.

The press reported that The Fox had achieved what only Sir Barton had previously done—won the Preakness, the Kentucky Derby, and the Belmont Stakes. One reporter said that the two horses might be called "Triple Event Winners." This is probably the first indication of the eventual designation, Triple Crown.

The racing fraternity moved to Saratoga in August, the scene of three of the greatest upsets in American racing. In 1919, Man o'War was defeated in the Sanford Memorial by a horse most aptly named Upset; in 1973 Secretariat lost to Onion in the Whitney Stakes; and 1930 saw Gallant Fox lose the Travers.

In the Travers, all attention was focused on the duel between Gallant Fox and Whichone, with nobody watching a mediocre race horse called Jim Dandy, who had started nineteen times that year without a win.

All during the race Whichone's rider and Earl Sande jockeyed for position, changing places back and forth in the heavy going and concentrating only on each other. So intent were they that, when Whichone swung wide on the last turn taking The Fox with him, Jim Dandy slipped through on the inside and won by an unbelievable eight lengths over Gallant Fox.

It was gossiped that a New Yorker who could not resist the

100 to 1 odds on Jim Dandy bet $1,000 with a bookmaker to win and pocketed $100,000. Fearing for his life, he left Saratoga for New York and quickly deposited the cash in the nearest bank vault.

Belmont Park on September 6, 1930, saw another record achieved when Gallant Fox won the mile and five-eighths Lawrence Realization. Until that day the biggest American money winner had been Zev with $313,639; winning the Lawrence made The Fox's total $317,865.

He didn't win by much. James Butler's Questionnaire, under "Sonny" Workman, another first-class jockey, went to the front, closely followed by Gallant Fox. They fought it out down the stretch and, in a tremendous drive, The Fox won by a head.

September 17, 1930, was Gallant Fox's last appearance of his racing career. Mr. Fitz chose the prestigious Jockey Club Gold Cup for the grand finale, and The Fox's easy victory showed that he was indeed the best three year old of 1930.

RACING RECORD

Year	Age	Starts	1st	2nd	3rd	Earnings
1929	2	7	2	2	2	$ 19,890
1930	3	10	9	1	0	308,275
	Totals	17	11	3	2	$328,165

Gallant Fox raced ten times at three, winning nine and losing only once, to Jim Dandy. His earnings for the year were $308,275. In his two years of racing, he started seventeen times with eleven firsts, three seconds, two thirds, and only once out of the money, for a total of $328,165.

Now that Gallant Fox was the leading American money winner, racing fans questioned whether he also led the rest of the world. The French Ksar was listed as winning $335,340, but under the European system, breeders' awards and the value of the trophies were added to the total. The Jockey Club computed Gallant Fox's earnings by the European method and, when they had added the worth of the various gold cups and breeders' awards, The Fox's total was raised to $341,365.

His fame was celebrated in many ways. One of the better-known Prohibition speakeasies in New York was called The Gallant Fox Club, but Mr. Woodward did not frequent it.

Gallant Fox was "unwound" over the next five weeks. He had been brought up to a peak of physical fitness and, as horse people say, he was "tight as a drum." Like any highly trained athlete, he had to relax gradually.

He returned to his birthplace, Claiborne Farm, then as now the largest thoroughbred stud farm in the world. Although he sired two great horses—Omaha, the American Triple Crown Winner, and Flares, Omaha's full brother and winner of the Ascot Gold Cup—the rest of his progeny was disappointing.

The Fox died at Claiborne, twenty-four years after his Triple Crown win, on the same day as the running of the Gallant Fox Handicap at Jamaica, and the Marguerite Stakes, named after his dam, at Pimlico. He was buried in the graveyard behind the Claiborne Farm office. There the headstones read like a "Who's Who" of racing: Johnstown, *Blenheim II, Nasrullah, Princequillo, Court Martial, Bold Ruler, *Sir Gallahad III, and his greatest son, Gallant Fox.

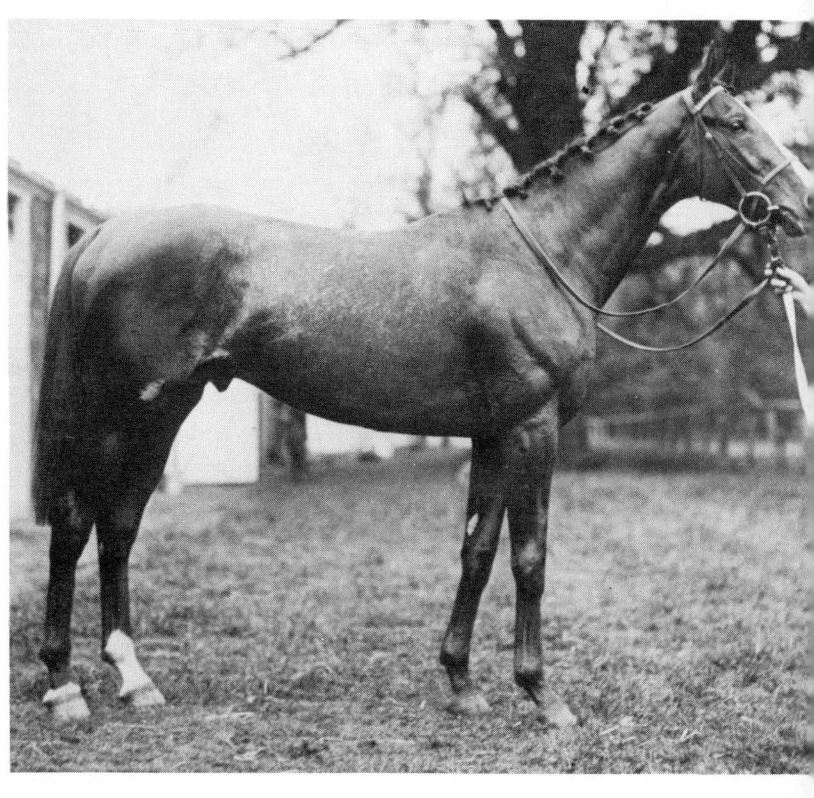

OMAHA (1932–1959)	*GALLANT FOX, 1927*	*°Sir Gallahad III*
		Marguerite
	FLAMBINO, 1924	*°Wrack*
		°Flambette

The Fox left behind a living monument, his son, Omaha, a big high-strung chestnut who, like his daddy before him, was born at Claiborne.

Following in the family tradition, he spent his babyhood at Claiborne, went to nursery school at Belair and, as a two year old, was sent to Mr. Fitz's school at Belmont, New York. There he was prepared for his lot in life—to become a high-class racing machine.

Omaha wasn't an easy pupil. Later, Mr. Fitz said that he was the most excitable colt he had ever handled.

In June of 1934, his two-year-old year, Omaha ran in his first race at Aqueduct. He came in second, but he broke his maiden in a five-furlong sprint a short week later.

With the rest of Mr. Fitz's gang he went to Saratoga for the month of August. Both men and horses enjoy the historic, tree-shaded track at the famous spa. The horses may not drink Saratoga's special waters, or take the medicinal baths, but the grass is greener to nibble on than at Belmont, and the air away from New York City is cleaner.

The colt's performance at Saratoga, and also on his return to Belmont, was only fair, and he ended his two-year-old season with one first, four seconds, and four times unplaced. He had won an unimpressive $3,850, but Mr. Fitz had hopes that he might turn into another stayer like his daddy.

Omaha's three-year-old year, 1935, was different. He started in a preparatory race at Jamaica on April 22 and scored the second win of his career.

He was impressive enough to be entered in the Wood Memorial, where he finished third behind two horses he had met the previous year—Today and Plat Eye—owned by a gaggle of Whitneys.

Omaha was sent by train to Churchill Downs for the Kentucky Derby on May 4, 1935. As he chugged toward Louisville, he was a very different colt from the youngster who had left Claiborne Farm a short two and a half years earlier. He had grown and filled out and was now a nice-looking chestnut—a little long in the back, but large and powerful. His manners had also improved. Running had given him a purpose in life and he was able to relax in his stall while those dancing attendance around him took part in the typical pre-Derby madness which envelops Louisville annually during the first few days of May.

Derby Saturday finally arrived with intermittent rain. This influenced the betting enough to make Calumet Farm's Nellie Flag, Eddie Arcaro's first Derby mount and a good "mudder," the favorite although she was a filly. Omaha's strong finishes, as yet unproductive, still made him second favorite for the mile-and-one-quarter classic.

Dr. Floyd Sager, now chief veterinarian at Claiborne, recalls that he met Mr. Woodward before the race and asked about Omaha's chances. Woodward minimized his colt's ability. "He may go wide at the turns," he told Sager. "He'll lose too much time to win."

Willie "Smokey" Saunders, Omaha's jockey, had other ideas as the eighteen horses started. Smokey Saunders held Omaha back and was soon in good position in the center of the track. After the first half-mile Saunders eased his hold on the big chestnut and, in an overwhelming burst of speed, Omaha took the lead. His long smooth stride devoured the ground, and with no apparent effort he crossed the finish line first. Nellie Flag, ridden by a young newcomer named Arcaro, was fourth.

Saunders was jubilant. "Omaha is the best horse I've ever

ridden," he said afterwards. "I had only to cluck to him when it was time to go to the front. My whip was just so much excess baggage."

This was a tremendous win for Smokey Saunders, Mr. Fitz's contract jockey. Born in Montana, the twenty-year-old lad had come a long way from galloping horses on the leaky roof circuit.

Saunders's nickname hailed from his first riding job. As an apprentice jockey, aged sixteen, he worked for a trainer who was death on smoking and drinking. One afternoon, clouds of smoke came out of the trainer's tack room. Thinking it was on fire, the foreman rushed over. It was only Willie Saunders puffing on a big cigar. Still today, working as a racing official in Florida, Saunders is known as "Smokey," rather than by his given name, William.

Winning the Derby put Saunders and Omaha in the limelight. It was immediately realized that the chestnut out of Gallant Fox's first crop of foals was potentially a great horse, and the betting public made him their favorite for the Preakness one week later.

For the first time since 1877, both houses of Congress adjourned early so that the members could go to Baltimore for the race. A crowd of forty thousand gathered under a clear sky as a field of eight horses paraded in front of the grandstand.

Omaha took the excitement in his stride. He kicked up his heels a little going to the post, but Saunders had no problems.

The start was good and Omaha moved up from sixth to fourth in the first half-mile. By the final turn he had bettered his position and then, repeating his Derby performance, he accelerated into the stretch, effortlessly opening up a six-length lead. He won at a slow gallop, with Saunders sitting still on his back. Nevertheless, the colt was only $\frac{2}{5}$ of a second off the track record of 1:58.

Omaha was shipped to New York and entered in the Withers Stakes. It was a disappointment, for Saunders lost ground by swinging wide—the problem that Woodward had worried about in the Derby—and Omaha was defeated by Willy du Pont's Rosemont.

The Belmont was next and the press speculated on whether Omaha could do what only his sire, Gallant Fox, and Sir Barton had accomplished: add the Belmont Stakes to his two previous victories. Despite Rosemont's Withers victory, Omaha went to the post as the favorite of the five entries.

After a slow start, Omaha stayed in the field and was fourth at one mile. He moved up on Firethorn in the stretch, with Rosemont running third. The famous Omaha "stretch kick"—a surge of speed in the final eighth of a mile—took the Belair colt over the finish line first with Rosemont third. It was a popular victory, and Mr. Woodward braved the heavy rain to lead in his second winner of the Triple Crown. Woodward became the first owner, and Sunny Jim Fitzsimmons the first trainer, in the history of American racing to have two Triple Crown winners. Since Woodward and Fitzsimmons had gotten together in 1923, they had won almost every major race in the East. The wealthy banker and the ex-poor boy from Brooklyn did not mind the drenching rain during the Belmont presentation ceremonies. This was their greatest moment!

Mr. Woodward began to plan for Omaha's future. He decided that the colt would finish out his victorious three-year-old year in the States, and would then be shipped to England to run in the prestigious 1936 Ascot Gold Cup.

Ever since his days at the American Embassy in London,

Woodward had raced in England, and it was just as important to him to have one of his horses win an English classic as to make a clean sweep of the American Triple Crown.

On January 8, 1936, Omaha sailed for England on the luxurious *Aquitania* in a special box stall befitting a Triple Crown winner. After a good sea voyage, he was immediately vanned to Newmarket.

The press gave him favorable notices and his English trainer, Captain Cecil Boyd-Rochfort, wrote, "He is such a nice-tempered horse and he gave us no trouble whatsoever." Omaha had changed markedly since his tempestuous yearling year.

Mr. Fitz ("Sunny Jim" Fitzsimmons) rated Omaha as the most excitable colt he had ever handled.

Omaha quickly settled down to training on historic Newmarket Heath, where racing first started under King James I in 1615. The chestnut enjoyed jogging and galloping over the miles of manicured grass. It was a change, and a pleasant one, from the dirt track at Belmont.

By May 9 he was ready for his first race, the one-and-one-half-mile Victor Wild Stakes at Kempton Park. Favored at 4 to 5 in the betting, and carrying 129 pounds, Omaha was held snugly for the first mile and then, in typical style, he opened up and, in a tremendous burst of speed, won with ease.

On May 30, the American invader challenged Lord Derby's Bobsleigh in the Queen's Plate at Kempton Park. Omaha carried 130 pounds to Bobsleigh's 123, and the two-mile race was run in a downpour. The leaders set a slow pace and the English jockey, Pat Beasley, later complained that his wrists ached from holding Omaha back for the first part of the race. Bobsleigh made his move after covering one and one-half miles, but Omaha stayed ahead of him to win. As Beasley dismounted he exclaimed, "What a colt!"

The greatest race meeting in the world was the next stop for our American visitor, for, to this day, Royal Ascot is the most splendid of English race meetings. A historic course, Ascot is adjacent to Windsor Castle, and, each day of racing, the reigning monarch drives to the races in an open carriage, drawn by four Windsor grays ridden by bewigged postilions in royal livery.

Black or gray top-hats are worn by the gentlemen in the royal enclosure, and the ladies are in colorful prints and their best spring hats—a far cry from the julep-drinking, casually dressed, infield crowd at Churchill Downs.

James R. Keene's Foxhall in 1882 was the first and only

American-bred horse to win the coveted Ascot Gold Cup, and William Woodward wanted his horse to be the second. Omaha had made a clean sweep of the United States Triple Crown and, if he could now win the Ascot Gold Cup, he would be sent to stud as the most famous race horse on both sides of the Atlantic.

With two impressive English wins behind him, Woodward's chestnut was the best American hope since 1882. His competition, in the pre-race analysis, was the Earl of Derby's Plassy, but Plassy was scratched. Lord Derby's family was still represented, however, by Derby's son, Lord Stanley, who entered his filly, Quashed. She had been winner of the filly classic, The Oaks, the previous year and was reputed to have the great staying power necessary for the two-and-one-half-mile classic.

Between 150,000 and 200,000 people gathered at England's most fashionable course. Court mourning for the late King George V prevented the appearance of King Edward VIII, who was to give up his crown several months later for "the woman I love" and become the Duke of Windsor.

The English track was different from anything in America. The horses ran clockwise, opposite to the States, and the grass course was irregular with alternating sharp and sweeping turns over the two and one-half miles, part of which was uphill.

Omaha seemed restless and sweated profusely in the paddock before the race. Jockey Beasley and Omaha had established rapport in past races and, with Beasley in the saddle, Omaha seemed to relax. The start was good and Beasley, on Omaha, and Perryman, on Quashed, stayed in the middle of the field of nine, each knowing that the real competition was from the other horse. The last quarter-mile was unforgettable as these two indomitable thoroughbreds matched stride for stride as if tied to each other. The finish was so close that no one but the judges clearly saw the result—Quashed won by a nose in what today would have been a photo-finish. Omaha had done his best in the most thrilling finish in the history of the Ascot Gold Cup. *Irish Field* magazine suggested that Quashed and Omaha be mated, but that was not to be.

The American colt was not through with English racing. On July 2 he ran at Newmarket in the mile-and-one-half Prince of Wales Stakes. His competition was the Aga Khan's Taj Akbar, who had placed second in the English Derby. Omaha had a great weight disadvantage; he carried 138 pounds to Taj Akbar's 120, and even Omaha could not overcome this handicap. The last quarter-mile was a repetition of the Ascot Gold Cup—a two-horse battle down the stretch with Omaha one neck behind Taj Akbar.

He rested through the winter and then resumed training at Newmarket for another attempt at the Ascot Gold Cup. In June it was announced that he had injured the tendon in his left foreleg, and he was to be shipped back to the States for stud duty at his birthplace, Claiborne Farm.

RACING RECORD

Year	Age	Starts	1st	2nd	3rd	Earnings
1934	2	9	1	4	0	$ 3,850
1935	3	9	6	1	2	142,255
1936	4	4	2	2	0	8,650
	Totals	22	9	7	2	$154,755

He came home a hero, but by 1943 it was apparent that this great horse was a failure at stud. Instead of retiring him, Mr. Woodward leased Omaha to The Jockey Club's Lookover Stallion Station at Avon, New York. By 1950, the Stallion Station no longer wanted him and he was sent to a farm near Omaha, Nebraska. There he was bred to any mare who would have him for a twenty-five dollar charitable donation—quite a comedown for a Triple Crown winner!

In 1952, the Ak-Sar-Ben (Nebraska spelled backwards) racecourse near Omaha, Nebraska, named a stakes race the Omaha Handicap. Like a pensioner on an outing, the old boy left the farm, all brushed, polished, and braided and, immediately before the running of the race named for him, paraded in front of the grandstand. His back was a little swayed, his eyes had that slightly sunken "old horse" look, but as the spectators applauded his appearance, he pranced a little and swished his famous chestnut tail.

Omaha, the third Triple Crown winner, died seven years later and was buried, not with the all-time greats at Claiborne Stud, but near his own monument at the Ak-Sar-Ben racecourse in far off Omaha, Nebraska.

WAR ADMIRAL (1934–1959)	*MAN o' WAR, 1917*	*Fair Play*
		Mahubah
	BRUSHUP, 1929	*Sweep*
		Annette K.

5
War Admiral
The Little Seal-Brown Colt

War Admiral, Man o'War's greatest son, did not inherit his father's size and magnificent presence, but he did receive what was most important, Man o'War's speed and will to win. War Admiral won the Triple Crown in 1937, the third horse since Sir Barton to do so. He topped Man o'War's earning record, and at stud he led the sires' list.

War Admiral lived and died in his father's shadow, but if it had not been for Man o'War, his owner Samuel Doyle Riddle might never have purchased Faraway Farm near Lexington, Kentucky, or gone so heavily into the breeding of thoroughbreds. Then, of course, there would have been no War Admiral.

Sam Riddle was the heir to a textile empire founded by his grandfather. A graduate of Swarthmore College, Riddle went into the family business, but the Riddle name was to become much more famous in racing circles than it had ever been in industry.

Before the turn of the century, Sam Riddle fox-hunted and rode in jumping races in Chester County, Pennsylvania, a longtime hunting and steeplechasing center. A thorough sportsman, Riddle gravitated naturally to the ownership of flat racers. Wealthy enough not to worry about his horses' earning their keep, he told his jockey and trainer that he expected the best horse to win. Riddle naturally hoped the best horse would be wearing the black and gold colors of Glen Riddle Farm, the name he gave to his racing stable.

Mr. Riddle went into flat racing in the 1890s, but didn't have his first stakes winner until 1916. He became increasingly active in racing and in 1918 made the buy of the century. He acquired the sixth-highest-priced colt at the Saratoga sales, a yearling named Man o'War, who gave his owner twenty stakes-winners as well as lasting fame.

But Man o'War's racing records, however impressive, make dull reading compared to his groom's glowing tribute to him. "He's got everything a hoss ought to have," said Will Harbut, "and he's got it where a hoss ought to have it. He is the mostest hoss." Much of "everything a hoss ought to have" was passed on to Man o'War's son, War Admiral.

In 1921, Sam Riddle and his nephew-in-law, Walter Jeffords, Sr., jointly started Faraway Farm, home of their stud, near Lexington, Kentucky. Faraway was in the heart of the bluegrass country, the greatest thoroughbred breeding center in the United States. Compared to other stud farms in the area, theirs was a modest spread; but with Man o'War in residence, it became the number one tourist attraction in the state. Some fifty thousand visitors a year signed the guest book.

Although his racing days were past, Man o'War continued to rule Faraway Farm from his breeding shed. Even the governor of Kentucky, "Happy" Chandler, attended "Big Red's" twenty-first birthday party in 1938, and NBC carried the festivities on a nationwide hookup. A carrot-decorated cake was presented to the birthday boy, but it was a case of "you may nuzzle but not eat it." Will Harbut took no chances with his charge.

Unlike some owners who did not seem to care what happened to their great horses, Sam Riddle at age eighty set up a trust fund for Man o'War's old age; he was to outlive his great stallion by four years, however.

When Big Red, aged twenty-six, suffered a heart attack, the farm was closed to the public. Will Harbut died first, and within a month, so did Man o'War.

Today, tourists still come to pay homage to the horse who is buried near Faraway, on a plot of land deeded to the state of Kentucky. The well-known sculptor, Herbert Haseltine, was commissioned to execute an heroic bronze of Man o'War for his final resting place.

More than ten years before Man o'War's death, however, Harrie B. Scott, manager of Faraway Farm, picked Brushup, a Riddle mare, to be mated to the famous horse. Brushup looked like a pony and, standing as tall as she could, measured only 15 hands. She had raced three times as a two year old, with one second and one third, and although her bloodlines were good, Brushup seemed a queer choice to be bred to the powerful 16.2-hand Man o'War.

The result of this mating was War Admiral, foaled May 2, 1934. Mr. Riddle was unimpressed with the seal-brown colt. War Admiral was small, he never grew beyond 15.2½ hands, and he was a far cry in appearance from his sire, Big Red. Walter Jeffords, though, liked his uncle's colt, particularly the pedigrees that combined the American blood of Fair Play and Domino with the English line of John o'Gaunt. He toyed with the idea of proposing a swap to Riddle—War Admiral for a good-looking Jeffords' colt that Riddle had admired. He decided not to make the offer, feeling that his uncle would never forgive him if War Admiral ever turned into something special. War Admiral certainly did!

In 1936 War Admiral, saddled by George Conway, went to the races wearing the black and gold colors of Glen Riddle. Conway preferred horses to headlines. Like Sam Riddle, his boss for close to twenty-five years, Conway was a shy and retiring man who had little use for reporters.

He had started with horses as a youngster and had worked his way up from mucking out stalls to groom, foreman, and finally assistant trainer at the Eaton Stud in New Jersey. In 1918 he joined Glen Riddle Farms as assistant trainer to Louis Feustel. The timing was perfect, for among the youngsters to be broken that year at the Riddle training center in Berlin, Maryland, was the bold chestnut colt, Man o'War.

Conway became head trainer in 1925, in time to work with Man o'War's sons and daughters. Crusader, as handsome as his sire, was Conway's favorite. War Admiral, the little seal-brown colt, had to win the Triple Crown before Conway was convinced that he was the better horse.

A good equine psychiatrist, George Conway understood the often temperamental War Admiral and saddled him throughout his racing career. A typical Man o'War colt, War Admiral fought force with force, but was willing and cooperative if approached tactfully. He never liked that monster, the starting gate, and by his antics often caused races to be delayed. His dislike became so violent that he was frequently permitted to start outside the gate, a pampering no longer permissible. Now horses must pass a starting-gate test and, if too fractious, they are ruled off the track.

In April 1936, War Admiral made his two-year-old debut at Havre de Grace, Maryland and, like his sire, broke his maiden by winning his first race. By May 21, 1936, he had moved to Belmont and scored his second win.

The National Stallion Stakes on June 6 was another story. There he met Pompoon, who was to go on to become the best two-year-old of 1936. Pompoon won; War Admiral was third behind him and Fencing.

A coughing virus, which had no respect for man or beast, sidelined many horses during that summer, including War Admiral. He was out of combat for ten weeks, never ran at Saratoga, and did not start again until the Eastern Shore Handicap at Havre de Grace on September 19. With Charles Kurtsinger up, he won ahead of Orientalist.

After a moderately successful two-year-old year, having won

Skittish at the starting gate, War Admiral usually took an early lead and kept it right down to the wire.

three of his six starts, War Admiral retired to winter at the Glen Riddle training center in Maryland.

The start of War Admiral's three-year-old year was most auspicious. In April 1937 he easily won a six-furlong race at Havre de Grace, prepping for the one-and-one-sixteenth-mile Chesapeake Stakes on April 24.

The Chesapeake, an important Kentucky Derby trial, saw War Admiral entered against Fairy Hill, the Santa Anita Derby winner, and Court Scandal, winner in Florida of the Flamingo. Charley Kurtsinger was again up, and War Admiral held the lead for the first six furlongs. At the top of the stretch Kurtsinger let out a notch and War Admiral drew away and won easily, with Court Scandal a poor second.

War Admiral became an immediate favorite for the Kentucky Derby and Mr. Riddle, for the first and only time in his long racing career, decided to forget his objections to running a horse in that classic. He had always felt strongly that a mile and a quarter at 126 pounds was too much to ask of a three year old so early in the season. To Mr. Riddle, racing was a hobby and not a business. Worried about the welfare of his horses, he would much rather have skipped a race than ask too much of a youngster.

War Admiral was fit and ready, and the excitement and tension around his stall at Churchill Downs did not bother him. The colt rested well before the running of the eighty-third Kentucky Derby.

Charles Kurtsinger, his jockey, was not that calm. Born within a Derby's length of Churchill Downs, Kurtsinger was the son of a small-time jockey. "Little Dutch," as Charley was called, began his racing career in 1923 and won his first Derby on Twenty Grand eight years later.

His lifelong ambition was to equal the record of three Derby victories shared by Earl Sande and Isaac Murphy, the great black jockey, and maybe this Derby was to be the second step on the ladder.

It rained torrents during the days just before the race and the prospect was for heavy going. But, by noon of D-day, the skies cleared, the weather turned swelteringly hot, and the track was fast.

The Derby was already on its way to becoming a major annual happening. Seventy-five thousand spectators engulfed Churchill Downs that day, but the infield crowd came to drink and have a party—seeing the race was secondary.

War Admiral was his usual fractious self and wanted no part of the starting gate. With the help of three other horses who were probably infected by his skittishness, he held up the race for eight minutes. Twenty horses started, close to the maximum number consistent with safety.

Too many entries have often been a problem at the Derby. Some owners are willing to pay the high entry fees for the status symbol of having ". . . run my horse in the Derby." As recently as 1974, there were so many nominations that the Derby was almost run in two sections, which would have destroyed the tradition of the Triple Crown.

Just before the 1974 race, the Kentucky Racing Commission ruled that twenty-four would be the absolute limit. Twenty-three started—still too many for good racing and safety. Little Current, later the Preakness and Belmont winner, was boxed in during the cavalry charge and lost his very good chance of winning the Triple Crown.

All of this crowding and jostling applied as well in 1937, and

War Admiral, in Post Position One, was most vulnerable. Fortunately, his usual quick start took him to the lead.

Under a snug hold War Admiral and Kurtsinger were still in the lead at the head of the stretch, where Pompoon, who had beaten War Admiral the previous year, made his bid. It was to no avail. Kurtsinger shook up his mount, drew away to a one-and-three-quarter-length victory over Pompoon, and gave Sam Riddle his first Derby.

Mr. Riddle was not at Churchill Downs that day. Confined by illness to his home in Glen Riddle, Pennsylvania, he listened to Clem McCarthy broadcast the Derby on radio.

George Conway, War Admiral's trainer, accepted the trophy from Governor "Happy" Chandler. The press tried to interview Mr. Riddle at home, but the shy and retiring sportsman was unavailable.

Mr. Riddle was besieged with offers to buy War Admiral, but he remained firm in his policy of never setting a price on one of his great horses. No amount would tempt him. To one persistent buyer Sam Riddle said, "If you owned War Admiral, would you sell him?" The answer was no.

The Derby victor was shipped to Baltimore and the Preakness by rail. Horse vans were little used before World War II, and sending horses by air was as far removed from reality as the submarine in Jules Verne's *Twenty Thousand Leagues Under the Sea.*

In the Preakness, Pompoon was again War Admiral's principal rival. Among the eight starters were two other sons of Man o'War, Over the Top and Walter M. Jeffords's Matey, both bred at Faraway Farm.

As usual, War Admiral was a bad boy at the gate, but after a four-minute delay the race began and he quickly took the lead. Kurtsinger allowed the colt to swing wide at the first turn, losing ground. Wayne Wright pushed Pompoon into the gap and gamely fought it out down to the homestretch. War Admiral prevailed by a head.

The Belmont in June was a special triumph for War Admiral. Hurt at the start, he still set a new American record of 2:28⅗ for one and one-half miles.

War Admiral got away fast, but stumbled badly and almost went down. He had "grabbed" himself (horse parlance for treading on his own right forefoot), an injury that might have stopped a lesser competitor. But he still drove forward. Challenged first by John Hay Whitney's Flying Scot and then by Maxwell Howard's Sceneshifter, War Admiral won easily. Blood-spattered but victorious, he entered the winner's circle.

The little seal-brown colt had gained the Triple Crown and accomplished what his sire, Man o'War, had not been given the opportunity to do. Deliberately not entered in the Kentucky Derby, Man o'War missed his chance to follow Sir Barton as the second winner of the Triple Crown.

After War Admiral's victory, Matt Winn of Churchill Downs suggested that his track join with Pimlico and Belmont to award $50,000 to every winner of these three races. Alfred Vanderbilt, at Pimlico, vetoed the idea. In 1950 the Thoroughbred Racing Associations began awarding Triple Crown Trophies, but a cash award has never been made.

Much of the credit for War Admiral's Triple Crown victory rightfully went to Charley Kurtsinger. Most experts agree that without a top jockey, few horses would ever enter the winner's circle. Kurtsinger, a superb rider, more than contributed his share. Like Eddie Arcaro and Citation, Milo Valenzuela and Kelso, Ron Turcotte and Secretariat, Charles Kurtsinger and War Admiral were a winning team.

The Belmont injury earned War Admiral a four-month vacation. He did not race again until he won at Laurel, Maryland, in October. It wasn't an important race, but it announced to the racing fraternity that the champ was back.

War Admiral was king of the East, but in California, Charles Howard's Seabiscuit reigned. A grandson of Man o'War, Seabiscuit had been waging a see-saw battle with War Admiral for the position of leading money winner.

If ever a race horse deserved to be called a "war horse" it was Seabiscuit. Seemingly stuck together with adhesive tape and safety pins, he was campaigned heavily as a two year old by "Sunny Jim" Fitzsimmons. "Mr. Fitz," trainer for both the prestigious Wheatley and Belair Stables, had so many good horses that he was happy to sell the mediocre Seabiscuit to Californian Charles Howard for $7,500. For Fitzsimmons, Seabiscuit had started forty-seven times, and won only nine unimportant races, earning $18,465.

For Charles Howard, California's largest automobile dealer, he became the leading money winner. Seabiscuit was the perfect example of a late bloomer, winning his great races as a four- and five-year-old. Whether it was the California sunshine, a different trainer, or Howard's golden touch, Seabiscuit came into his own on the West Coast. In the East, at three, he was not Triple Crown material and was not entered in any of the Triple Crown races.

Steadily, as Seabiscuit won or placed in good races, he and War Admiral became contenders for top honors. A head-on confrontation was set for the Washington Handicap but

Seabiscuit was scratched, leaving War Admiral with an easy victory.

The Pimlico Special ended the 1937 season for War Admiral. He won the race, but Kurtsinger did not like the way the colt ran, and there was some speculation that War Admiral had "gone wrong" and would be retired. Mr. Riddle announced that both the colt and George Conway were to take a two-month vacation. In January, all rumors were set to rest when Mr. Riddle sent George Conway and War Admiral to Hialeah for the winter racing. War Admiral won in Florida and, once again, a possible match between War Admiral and Seabiscuit became racing's most talked-about subject. Everyone remembered the 1920 race at Kenilworth in Canada between Man o'War and Sir Barton, and the principal tracks in the country were soon bidding for a match.

A $100,000 purse at Belmont Park was suggested, while John D. Hertz was offering a like amount for Chicago's Arlington Park, and Boston's Suffolk Downs was ready with its proposal of $50,000. None of the offers was accepted and another "race of the century" was not run.

Both horses were entered in the Massachusetts Handicap at Suffolk Downs, but the track was heavy and, just before the race, Seabiscuit was withdrawn on a veterinarian's certificate. War Admiral was the overwhelming favorite, but he proved that every good horse has a bad race in him and came in fourth to Hal Price Headley's bay colt, Menow. During the race, War Admiral again "grabbed" himself, and this may have contributed to his defeat, his first loss after eleven straight victories.

He was in form again by August for Saratoga, winning the Saratoga Handicap, the Whitney Stakes, and the Saratoga

Cup. Back in New York, he won the weight-for-age Jockey Club Gold Cup at two miles.

When practically all hope of a War Admiral-Seabiscuit race had been lost, Samuel Riddle and Charles Howard, urged on by Alfred Gwynne Vanderbilt, then vice-president of the Maryland Jockey Club, signed an agreement to race the two horses against each other at Pimlico.

The contract was a most formal undertaking. The race, on November 1, 1938, was to be at equal weights of 120 pounds over one and three-sixteenths miles. Each owner put up a $5,000 guarantee to be forfeited if his horse did not start. The track was to be inspected at 8:30 A.M. on the morning of the race by a "neutral person," and if he decided the track was muddy the race would be postponed. Neither horse liked heavy going.

The Pimlico management put up a $15,000 purse, winner take all. After the $100,000 races offered by both Belmont Park and Arlington Park, it may be hard to understand why Riddle and Howard would settle for $15,000; however, the two sportsmen were both extremely wealthy, money was secondary, and Pimlico probably fitted in with their plans.

Then the ballyhoo started. A publicity booklet was published by Pimlico for the press, containing records and descriptions of the horses and the history of racing in Maryland. It also had a fascinating bit of inconsequential historical minutia: a 1789 expense accounting by George Washington detailing his racing losses at £1/6s, his winnings at cards of £13, and his expenses for two cases of wine, £25.

Before the race, the most popular betting was that it would never happen, but November 1 dawned clear, the track was fast, and the race was on. Forty thousand people jammed into

Pimlico as the horses went to the post. In those days before television, the race was broadcast on radio by NBC's Clem McCarthy.

To please Mr. Riddle, who held Pimlico starter James Milton in low esteem, George Cassidy was imported from New York. It was a walk-up start and, on the third attempt, they were off.

There are two kinds of thoroughbreds: front-runners and come-from-behind horses. Throughout his career, War Admiral was the former. In this race, for almost the first time, another horse got away from the start faster than War Admiral, and that spelled trouble. Seabiscuit, ridden by "The Iceman," George Woolf, outran him down the stretch and was on the rail, two lengths ahead of War Admiral at the first turn. The son and grandson of Man o'War battled head and head until they were well into the homestretch, but in the last furlong Seabiscuit drew away to a four-length victory. He ran the one and three-sixteenths miles in $1{:}56\frac{3}{5}$, setting a new track record. Seabiscuit became the king of the handicap division.

War Admiral's last race as a four year old was the Rhode Island Handicap at Narragansett on November 12, 1938. Again fractious, he was started outside the gate but had no trouble putting away Mucho Gusto and Busy K.

In three years of racing, War Admiral, promising as a two year old, had become a Triple-Crown-winning three-year-old, and by four dominated the handicap division. He missed being named Horse of the Year when Seabiscuit, the challenger from the West, beat him in the Pimlico Special.

War Admiral settled down for a rest at Glen Riddle Farms until January 1939 when he was sent to Florida to get ready for the Widener Handicap at Hialeah. In February he was entered in a preparatory race in which he beat Pasteurized. After the race, he developed a fever and was sent north.

In May 1939 it was reported that War Admiral had wrenched an ankle, which took him out of training, and in June he was officially retired from racing. In ill health for most of War Admiral's four-year-old year, trainer George Conway died after War Admiral had discarded his running shoes. Although as reticent about his age as he was about War Admiral's prowess, George Conway was in his seventies when he died.

RACING RECORD

Year	Age	Starts	1st	2nd	3rd	Earnings
1936	2	6	3	2	1	$ 14,800
1937	3	8	8	0	0	166,500
1938	4	11	9	1	0	90,840
1939	5	1	1	0	0	1,100
	Totals	26	21	3	1	$273,240

War Admiral was retired to stud at Faraway Farm, where his sire had stood for so many years. Mr. Riddle's decision to open his book to the public, rather than restrict him to family-owned mares, greatly helped War Admiral's record. From 1944 to 1958 he was among the twenty leading sires of North America and his get won $6,804,507.

Mr. Riddle died in 1951, aged ninety, and in September 1958 his broodmares, yearlings, and weanlings were sold to Rex Ellsworth. The Riddle portion of Faraway Farm was also sold, and the last four Glen Riddle stallions, War Admiral among them, were sent to stand at Hamburg Place in Lexington, the birthplace of the first Triple Crown winner, Sir Barton.

On the evening of October 29, 1959, War Admiral became ill in his stall at Hamburg Place. He died the next day and was laid to rest at the foot of Herbert Haseltine's magnificent statue of Man o'War. Thus, War Admiral was buried, as he lived, in the shadow of his sire, but the little seal-brown colt was indisputably the greatest son of that incredible horse, Man o'War.

WHIRLAWAY (1938–1953)	**BLENHEIM II, 1927*	*Blandford*
		Malva
	DUSTWHIRL, 1926	*Sweep*
		Ormonda

6
Whirlaway
Mr. Longtail

WHIRLAWAY, THE LITTLE CHESTNUT with the long, long tail won the Triple Crown in 1941 and started Calumet Farm on the road to becoming the greatest stable in the history of American racing. Citation, seven years later, carried the devil's red and blue Calumet colors to their all-time peak.

The two colts had the same owner, Warren Wright, Sr., the same Triple Crown jockey, Eddie Arcaro, and the same father-and-son trainer team of B. A. "Plain Ben" and H. A. "Jimmy" Jones. The winning ways of these two horses is the story of Warren Wright and Calumet Farm.

It all started with Warren Wright's mother, Mrs. William Monroe Wright. She loved to bake and was not satisfied with the baking powder available. When Mrs. Wright decided to make her own, it was so much better than the rest that the neighboring ladies clamored to use it. The demand became so great that William Wright decided to market his wife's product in the Calumet section of Chicago's South Side.

Mr. Wright went from house to house, ringing doorbells and selling his wares. The Fuller Brush man and the Avon lady may enjoy making house calls, but Wright did not. Years later, he told a friend that he became so disgusted with the project that he would happily have sold his wife's baking powder recipe for $100.

As the business expanded, William Wright needed a trade name for the baking powder. He called it Calumet, after the district where it had first been sold. Calumet was an Indian word for "pipe of peace," and the head of an Indian chief soon became a familiar figure on every can.

Like the more recent Margaret Rudkin, whose home baking grew into the giant Pepperidge Farm enterprise, Mrs. Wright's baking powder blossomed into an enormous business. The company was sold in 1928, on the eve of the Great Depression, for close to $30 million.

William Monroe Wright, like many midwesterners, was interested in trotting horses. Now a rich man, he bought a horse farm on the outskirts of Lexington, in the heart of Kentucky's bluegrass country.

Calumet Butler, the first of many great Calumet horses, won the Hambletonian, the trotting horse equivalent of the Kentucky Derby, in 1931. That same year William Wright's son, Warren, whose interest was in thoroughbreds rather than standardbreds, bought three yearlings at the Saratoga sales. He named them Flirting, Lucille Wright, and Warren, Jr. The horses were raced in 1932 and had one first, one second, and two thirds—with total winnings of $1,150. This was a small beginning for the stable that, in the next forty years, was to win more than $21 million.

Short and dapper, with gray hair and rimless glasses, Warren Wright was the picture of the successful businessman. He had sold the baking powder company at the top of the market. He bought land in Texas and found oil. He turned a hobby—racing—into a big business. He demanded perfection, an according to Margaret Glass, longtime office manager anc watchdog at Calumet, "Mr. Wright usually had his way."

Vitally interested in every phase of racing, Mr. Wright made Calumet Farm the showplace of the Kentucky breeding establishments. He opened it to the public and, at the farm office, visitors were given a map and were free to wander around the beautiful acres. According to Mrs. Glass, the first guest appeared the Sunday after "Whirly" won the Derby and, over the years, thousands came to pay homage to the equine stars.

On the Sunday after the 1948 Derby, visitors caused the granddaddy of all traffic jams at Calumet. Everyone wanted to see Citation's home, and traffic came to a standstill on the narrow farm roads. The Calumet staff was swamped, and both city and county police had to be called in to unsnarl the cars.

In the 1960s, a rash of barn fires on stud farms near Lexington caused owners to take a hard look at the droves of visitors who took advantage of the "open gate" policy. Regretfully, like most of the other farms, Calumet closed its gates to the general public. Today, visitors pass through the impressive white entrance "by invitation only."

Calumet's 846 acres of bluegrass is divided by twenty-three miles of white oak fencing and six miles of private roads. The main residence, the office, and more than thirty-five stables, barns, and sheds are painted white with brilliant devil's red trim. Not a blade of grass is left unmowed and a crew of painters continually fights the battle against tattletale gray.

Behind the farm office, with its red-and-white striped awnings, is the stallion barn with a one-acre paddock for each stallion in residence. Today, Tim Tam—the winner of the 1958 Derby and Preakness, and Forward Pass—the Derby and Preakness winner in 1968, look inquisitively over the fence, as did Bull Lea, the foundation sire and the greatest single reason for Calumet's success.

Bull Lea, possibly the foremost American sire of the twentieth century, was bought by Mr. Wright at the 1936 Saratoga sales for $14,000. After winning ten races and a more than respectable $94,825, he "bowed"—severely sprained a tendon in his leg—and was retired to Calumet, a fat cripple. His sons and daughters won more than $13,000,000.

Whirlaway, or "Mr. Longtail" as he was known to the working press, was not a Bull Lea colt; he was by the Aga Khan's English Derby winner, *Blenheim II. Imported by a syndicate for $250,000—a huge sum in the 1930s—*Blenheim II stood at A. B. Hancock, Jr.'s Claiborne Farm. Mr. Wright, showing his usual business acumen, had bought a one-quarter interest in this magnificently bred, but difficult, and at times downright crazy, stallion.

Whirlaway's dam, Dustwhirl, an unraced mare, was by Sweep, who also sired War Admiral's dam, Brushup. Through her dam's line, Dustwhirl's ancestry traced back to Ormonde, one of the winners of that greatest test in horse racing, the British Triple Crown.

Whirlaway was just a baby, running in the pastures of Calumet, when Wright hired Ben Jones to train his racing stable. Almost thirty years later, Ben Jones's son, Jimmy, still feels that, "If it hadn't been for Whirlaway, we might have gone back to Missouri."

Mr. Wright loved to win and when Calumet's Bull Lea, the second favorite for the 1938 Derby, finished more than seventeen lengths behind the winner, Lawrin, trained by Ben Jones, Warren Wright knew that Jones was his man.

Some say that Warren Wright had the Midas touch, others put it differently: "He knew how to pick key people." When he hired Ben Jones in 1939, he added the missing ingredient to his winning team, which for the next twenty-five years would make Calumet the greatest stable in the history of United States racing.

Whether called "B. A." or "Plain Ben," Jones is regarded by many as this country's greatest trainer. He was a genius at knowing a good horse and what to do with him. Born in 1882, near Parnell, Missouri, he grew up as a rancher's son and went to the college that later became Colorado A & M. He soon realized that an academic career was not for him. "I couldn't decide which I liked better, cattle or horses, but when I got big enough to help with the milking, I made up my mind."

Jones started training in a tough league, the "bush" tracks of the Southwest and Mexico. The races there were mostly sprints, sometimes only two to four hundred yards, and a half mile was a long run. It was a hand-to-mouth existence and Jones had to win lots of races to feed his family.

Nonetheless, Jones did all right in that harum-scarum life. He won races and did some breeding. He had acquired a well-bred stallion named Seth, who had the knack of siring good race horses out of indifferent mares. Seth was tied as the leading sire of two year olds in 1929, and was among the top twenty sires for the previous four years. All this helped pay the bills and, in the process, Ben Jones started to achieve a reputation.

In 1932, when Herbert M. Woolf asked Ben Jones to train for his Woolford Farm near Kansas City, Jones had his first chance to run high-priced horses at the bigger tracks. Woolf's horses did well, and in 1938, when Lawrin won the Derby, Jones hit the big time.

When Ben Jones, with his son Horace A. (Jimmy) as assistant, arrived at Calumet in 1939, Whirlaway was a yearling, ready to test the ability of any trainer. A problem colt, he had inherited from his sire, *Blenheim II, a slightly mad disposition. With enormous potential and blinding bursts of speed, he was always erratic and difficult. Probably no other trainer could have made Whirlaway into a Triple Crown horse.

Ben Jones decided early on that Whirlaway needed a mountain of work to keep him fit, and he was raced sixteen times as a two year old. He also needed a mountain of patience. He was a spooky horse, and Jones hand-walked him around every track he was asked to race on. Whirlaway's understanding trainer gave him a chance to stare at the jumps next to the flat track, snort at the grandstand, and sniff the starting gate. Familiarity with his surroundings, and blinkers, made him concentrate on runnng rather than looking.

"Whirly" broke his maiden the first time out, in a five-furlong sprint at Lincoln Fields, Chicago. Here he clearly indicated the pattern for the future—tremendous speed, but a nerve-racking habit of drifting to the outside rail. Ben Jones said later, "I knew he was a runner. . . . In his first race, at Lincoln Fields, he went to the outside fence, followed it around the entire five-eighths, and still came in first."

At Arlington Park, also in Chicago, he won one out of five races, and then moved on to Saratoga, New York, where he was second in the United States Hotel Stakes. Next came the prestigious Saratoga Special. He acted up in the paddock, nearly throwing his rider, Johnny Longden. The crowd loved his antics, but the critics watched him for a different reason—his remarkable finishing punch. Whirlaway, jammed in at the start, almost went down, but Longden pulled him together and went on to win with a devastating rush.

One turf writer compared his performance to that of his sire, *Blenheim II, in winning the English Derby. Some said that his tremendous burst at the end was bolting, not running, and that he was out of control. But it was apparent that Whirlaway, *Blenheim II's first American-bred stakes winner, was a colt to watch.

In the Hopeful, one of the great two-year-old races, the track was muddy, and the leading horses bore out to get away from the soft going close to the rail. Whirlaway's jockey could not hold him straight and Mr. Longtail drifted even further out. He looked hopelessly beaten until the stretch, when he suddenly became jet-propelled and came on with a rush through the mud and slop to win his biggest purse of the year, $37,850.

The October Breeders' Futurity at Keeneland was one of the fall races studied to determine the best two year old. At the track, which almost adjoins Calumet Farm, Whirly once again ran a characteristic race—trailing the field and then, with his usual show of finishing power, winning by a length going away.

In the Walden Stakes at Pimlico, the track was sloppy, but George Woolf managed to hold him straight and he won handily. Thus ended Whirlaway's first year of racing with sixteen starts, seven firsts, two seconds, four thirds, and total earnings of $77,275. A good year, not a great one, marked throughout by his erratic behavior.

"He's as nervous as a cat in a room full of rocking chairs," said Ben Jones, and his son, Jimmy, added, "He's a kind of a nut." But nutty or not, America's turf writers named him the two-year-old Horse of the Year.

Whirlaway had caught the imagination of the racing public. They loved to see Mr. Longtail come from behind, his tail, like the golden trail of a rocket, streaming after him. Ben Jones

Full of Derby-inspired confidence, Whirlaway and trainer Ben Jones arrived in Baltimore for the Preakness.

realized Whirlaway's potential and knew he had a horse of Derby caliber.

In 1943, short sprints were planned before the longer three-year-old Triple Crown classics. Mr. Wright, who rarely interfered, voiced his objection. "Why race a classic colt in sprint races?" In Florida for the winter, Wright wanted to see his colt run in the prestigious Flamingo Stakes. Jones felt that the mile and one-eighth of the Flamingo was too long and too soon.

Wright was insistent, but so was Jones. He could not flatly say no to his boss but, instead, the canny Missourian told Mr. Wright that Whirly had "popped a splint"—a bony swelling had appeared on his leg.

The usual treatment for a splint is a "blister," in which an irritating chemical compound is rubbed on the bump. This, like a mustard plaster, sets up heat in the leg, which increases the blood supply and helps heal the inflammation. The irritant has the effect of slightly burning the hair on the leg, and Jones treated the horse with enough of the compound to show some scorch marks, convincing Mr. Wright that the colt could not go in the Flamingo.

A few weeks later, with the splint miraculously healed, Whirlaway was entered in the five-and-one-half-furlong Silver Springs Purse at Tropical Park. Mr. Longtail won, and Warren Wright never again tried to second-guess his trainer.

From Florida he was shipped to Keeneland, the traditional proving ground of Derby hopefuls. He won the three-quarter mile A. J. Joyner Handicap and then attempted the Blue Grass Stakes, with Wendell Eads up. Eads, barely out of apprentice ranks, was the Calumet contract jockey. He could not hold the colt; Whirly bolted in the stretch and finished six lengths behind Our Boots.

The one-mile Derby Trial Stakes at nearby Churchill Downs, the week before the Kentucky Derby, was the last prelude to the "Run for the Roses." Whirlaway started slowly and stayed in fifth place for the first half-mile. He made his move, a run which some horsemen said was the fastest they had ever seen, and was leading by a half length coming into the stretch. At this crucial moment Eads, once again, could not hold him straight and Whirlaway bore out and lost the race. He could have won handily if he had not been up to his usual tricks but, at that, the time of 1:36⅗ was less than a second slower than the Churchill Downs record.

Jones now knew that in Whirlaway he had a potential superhorse, but only under the control of a super rider. So he called on the greatest of the great, Eddie Arcaro, who had won the 1938 Derby for him on Lawrin.

"Heady Eddie" Arcaro was small in stature as befits a jockey, but he towered in his profession. By the time he retired, the "Old Master" had won 4,779 races with purses totalling $30,039,543.

Ohio-born, Arcaro started as a stable boy at thirteen. He was soon exercising race horses and from this graduated to riding races. In the spring of 1933 he went to Chicago and soon acquired a reputation as an *enfant terrible.* He was brought up to believe that, as Leo Durocher once said about baseball, "nice guys finish last." Nothing was barred: straight-arming another jockey, grabbing an opponent's saddle cloth, or locking legs with the jockey alongside to throw him off balance. In the intervening years he had mellowed, but he never lost his competitive drive and was often suspended by the stewards for rough riding.

In 1941, with Whirlaway's chances in the Derby hanging in the balance, Jones needed Arcaro. B. A.'s analysis of the problem was twofold. First he wanted a rider with sympathetic "hands"—that magic touch, combined with the right amount of strength, which makes all horses "go well" for certain riders. This, he knew, Arcaro had. Secondly, there was Whirlaway's aversion to the inside rail. Here the true genius of Ben Jones became apparent.

As "Heady Eddie" tells the story: "B. A. took me out to the track to work the horse, and he said he would sit on his pony at the head of the stretch. I was to take Whirlaway between him and the rail.

"Well, I broke the horse off at the half-mile pole, and when I come around the turn I look up, and B. A. looks to me like he's sitting on top of the rail. I thought to myself, goddam, ole man, if you're game, I am."

This showed not only that Ben Jones and his pony had the courage to hold their ground while a thousand-pound horse charged down upon them at almost forty miles per hour, but it proved that Arcaro could keep Whirly straight. But Jones still had not solved the horse's aversion to the inside rail. B. A. had always run the colt in blinkers to keep his attention on the horses ahead but, minutes before the running of the Kentucky Derby, Jones made a far-reaching decision. Arcaro described what happened:

"I came down to the paddock before the race, and B. A.'s asking everyone around if they've got a pocketknife. Someone finally finds one for him, and right there he cut off the inside blinker. I said this was a helluva time to be experimenting, but B. A. says, 'Don't worry, it's gonna be all right.' "

The new team of Arcaro and Whirlaway, complete with one-eyed blinker, went to the Kentucky Derby starting gate the favorite with the betting crowd. They knew that he *could* win—but would he?

Before the start, Arcaro jogged Mr. Longtail up and down the track and, so as not to frighten the unpredictable favorite, the band cooperated and played the traditional "My Old Kentucky Home" softly. Horses like music, but loud noises panic them. Whirlaway acted up a bit for his fans, but settled down quickly for Arcaro.

The competition was keen. Louis Tufano's Market Wise, a $1,500 claimer who had become a stakes horse, and Blue Pair and Our Boots—both of whom had defeated Whirlaway in other races—were among the starters.

There was no problem at the gate. Whirlaway got away to a fast start, and Arcaro held him in about eighth place. Whirlaway was running smoothly, every stride a fluid motion. Slowly he moved to fourth place, two lengths behind the leader. Now came the real test; usually, at the homestretch turn, he would become unmanageable and lunge to the outside rail. Instead Whirlaway, obviously delighted with his new jockey and his new blinker, became jet-propelled and stormed ahead straight as an arrow, to win by eight lengths—one of the most decisive victories in the history of the Derby. He ran the mile and one-quarter in 2:01$\frac{2}{5}$, a track record which stood until Decidedly shaved off one second in the 1962 Derby twenty-one years later.

Decidedly's Kentucky Derby record of 2:00$\frac{2}{5}$ stood for two years until Northern Dancer, a grandson of Native Dancer, lowered it to 2:00 in 1964. Nine years later, 1973, Secretariat set still another record of 1:59$\frac{2}{5}$. It took thirty-two years to better Whirlaway's time by two seconds—a time set by a problem horse running his first good race.

Ben Jones, the taciturn midwesterner, said after the Derby, "He's just now getting good. He's not quite ready yet."

This reversal of form was not accepted at its face value by the cynical backstretch horsemen. Possibly looking for an excuse for their own horses, they spread a rumor that Whirlaway had been doped in the Florida races during the previous winter. The story even got into print, in Dan Parker's column in the *New York Mirror*. Although Parker retracted the story the next day, there was still some doubt that Whirlaway's victory in the Derby had not been helped by drugs.

All doubts were settled by the Preakness. Whirlaway ran best coming from behind, and Arcaro had so much confidence in him that he let him take his own time out of the starting gate. At the half-mile pole he was last, coasting about ten lengths behind the leader, King Cole, and then Arcaro turned him loose. He went around and through the cluster of horses ahead of him like a knife through ice cream and was first coming out of the turn into the stretch. This was the moment of truth.

Arcaro had to take Whirlaway well out toward the center of the track to get racing room, and the fatal fascination for the outside rail should have shown itself. Arcaro, his masterly hands playing with Whirlaway's mouth like a violin virtuoso, kept the colt straight, and Mr. Longtail won the Preakness by five and one-half lengths. In the jockey room after the race Eddie Arcaro said, "Wipe the jam off my mouth; I've been to a picnic."

Jones was jubilant. On the one hand he said "I will, if Mr. Wright approves, match Whirlaway against any three-year-old, anywhere," but he also called Whirlaway the "dumbest horse I've ever trained."

Jones considered Whirlaway dumb because he never learned that the steeplechase jumps alongside the track would not bite, that the noisy mob in the grandstand, who helped pay for his oats, would not hurt a hair of his beautiful long tail, and that the awesome machinery of the starting gate insured a fair start—and not the sudden death of a small chestnut colt called Whirlaway. Jones kept his part of the bargain; before every race, he personally took Whirly on an inspection trip of the course. Most of the time Mr. Longtail repaid his trainer's time and patience by winning.

Jones believed that Whirlaway was a glutton for work. Almost a month between the Preakness and the Belmont was too long for the colt to remain unraced. To keep him busy, Jones put Whirlaway in the mile and one-sixteenth Henry of Navarre Purse and Mr. Longtail won it.

By now it was obvious that he was the best three-year-old of 1941, and the betting public made him the favorite for the Belmont. The crowd loved him but the competition did not. Only three took up the challenge: J. F. Byers' colt Robert Morris, C. V. Whitney's Yankee Chance, and the King Ranch's Itabo.

The start was good for the one-and-one-half-mile classic and Arcaro, once again, played a waiting game. He stayed in third place for the first half-mile while the other jockeys set a slow pace, thinking that it might be the key to beating Whirlaway. Arcaro was having no part of this. He shouted to the other jockeys, "The hell with this, fellas, I'm leaving," as he turned

Mr. Longtail loose. A seven-length lead was quickly opened and Arcaro eased up on his mount. The rest of the race was a breeze, and Whirlaway was an easy victor of the Belmont Stakes.

He had won the big three, the Triple Crown that only four other horses had managed to win in the history of United States racing, but his owners, Mr. and Mrs. Warren Wright, were not at Belmont Park to accept the trophy. They were at Warren Jr.'s graduation at Denver University, and listened to the race on the radio. Mr. Wright, in newspaper interviews, graciously gave full credit to Ben Jones for making a great horse out of a problem child.

Whirlaway was to race nine more times that year. When Eddie Arcaro was not in the saddle, due to prior commitments or because of having been set down by the stewards, the colt sometimes reverted to his old habit of bearing out. This cost him a win in the third of these races, the Classic Stakes at Arlington Park.

He won his next three races and then came in second in the Narragansett Special. This time the problem was different. As usual, Whirly lagged behind at the start, but when it was time for his famous stretch run, it never came. War Relic, ridden by Ted Atkinson, finished four lengths ahead of Whirlaway.

Ben Jones and his assistant, son Jimmy, could not explain it. To Ben, "He looked as good as ever." The possibility that Whirlaway had been raced too much was answered by Jimmy. "Just the contrary. He needs work and plenty of it . . . I wish we could run him every Saturday."

The 1941 season was drawing to a close and the September 20 running of the Lawrence Realization, one and five-eighths miles at Belmont Park, was Whirlaway's next to last appearance for the year. Despite his disappointing performance in the Narragansett Special, Mr. Longtail was still the darling of the crowd. This time when his jockey, Robertson, opened up in the backstretch, Mr. Longtail came home an easy winner.

Comparing this race to Whirlaway's defeat at Narragansett, Ben Jones said he had allowed Whirlaway to do too much loafing prior to that race.

The Jockey Club Gold Cup, two miles at Belmont Park, was the Calumet colt's last race of the year. He was beaten by Market Wise, but it was an honorable defeat: a loss by a nose while Market Wise cut a full second off Exterminator's American record for two miles.

Whirlaway had emerged as an iron horse: twenty races during the year, never unplaced, with thirteen victories, five seconds, and two thirds. Most important, he was still sound and unblemished. He had swelled the Calumet coffers with $272,386 and a host of trophies, including those of the Triple Crown races and the plaque of Horse of the Year to add to his previous year's nomination as the best two-year-old.

Whirlaway was the big money-maker for Calumet in 1941, but the stable, greatly expanded by Ben Jones and his son Jimmy, was running horses on both the East and West coasts.

After the Jockey Club Gold Cup at Belmont, Whirlaway was shipped to California with two cars of Warren Wright's horses. Whirly was the star, and he was given star treatment. His constant stable companion, a white pony, kept him company on the long cross-country haul, and so did Pinky Brown, his exercise boy, and Dan Barnett, his groom.

More than three thousand people were on hand to see him arrive at Santa Anita. Every aspiring movie starlet tried to have her picture taken with Mr. Longtail. He was inclined to nip a little and show his heels, but he was a ham at heart and proved to be most cooperative with the photographers. Pearl Harbor, on December 7, 1941, ended racing at Santa Anita, and Whirlaway spent a quiet winter in California.

Wartime racing was spotty. Some tracks closed for the duration and others shortened their race meetings. As soon as nationwide gasoline rationing became a way of life, track attendance plummeted, but for the two-dollar bettor there was always a way. Count Fleet's 1943 Kentucky Derby was called the Street Car Derby and, as at Churchill Downs, some form of public transportation was always available to tracks all over the country. Although the crowds were smaller, racing continued.

Most stables raced throughout the war. Many, with owners, trainers, and help in the armed services, operated on a limited basis. Not so with Calumet. In the early forties Warren Wright often had sixty horses at the track, and another two hundred broodmares and youngsters at the farm.

As the 1942 season opened in a country at war, Whirlaway was a four year old. Many of the races open to him were handicaps. The handicapper tries to equalize the contestants' chances of victory by assigning the weights to be carried, based on his evaluation of each horse's ability. As one pound of weight is considered equal to one length at the finish, weight carried is of the utmost importance.

The struggle between the owner and his trainer, and the handicapper, has been going on as long as there have been handicap races. At the end of Man o'War's three-year-old year, his owner, Samuel D. Riddle, asked Walter S. Vosburgh, the famous handicapper, what weight Mr. Vosburgh would put on Man o'War at four. Mr. Vosburgh said, "If he wins his first race, I'll put the heaviest weight on him that any horse has carried in my lifetime."

Mr. Riddle refused to take the chance of breaking down his great colt by racing under excessive weights, and retired him as a three year old.

Today, with four-, five-, and six-million-dollar syndications for horses at stud, owners are afraid to risk injury to their valuable four-legged investments, and retire them from racing at the earliest possible moment.

Whirlaway was a work horse, and winning the Triple Crown did not give him a passport to a life of love and ease. He was to be raced twenty-two times, many of the races handicaps, in his four-year-old year. He ran against older horses, carrying punishing weights, but he won twelve of his races and was never out of the money.

Whirlaway had won the Triple Crown for Calumet, and now Warren Wright and Ben Jones had another goal. Seabiscuit, the great California stallion, by then retired, held the all-time earnings record of $437,730. Whirlaway's four-year-old campaign was aimed at topping this and then becoming the first $500,000 horse. Stud duty could wait.

Whirly entered his fourth year with close to $350,000 in the bank. With half a dozen big money races available to four year olds, it seemed almost certain that the Calumet colt would surpass the California horse if he stayed sound. A horse can go unsound in a moment. A tendon in the leg can rupture, or a bone in the foot shatter, in an instant while the horse is galloping. This is the sword of Damocles hanging over every trainer's head.

Jones was more than justified in calling Whirly a nut, but he was a tough nut, and that was of utmost importance.

In March, he was shipped east. He was in the money in seven races and then he won the Brooklyn Handicap at Aqueduct. At one and one-quarter miles, it was a big race for Whirlaway. He stormed to the finish ahead of Greentree Stables' Swing and Sway and added $23,650 to his earnings. Whirlaway was now $33,244 behind Seabiscuit's money-winning world record.

The winner's share of the one-and-one-eighth-mile Massachusett's Handicap at Suffolk Downs would put Whirlaway ahead of Seabiscuit. Ridden by George Woolf, Whirlaway won going away, with a new track record of 1:48$\frac{1}{5}$. "Mr. Longtail's" total earnings were $454,336 and the position of Number One was his.

George Woolf, a great rider, whose life ended tragically in a riding accident at Santa Anita a few years later, was known as "The Iceman." Ultracool and collected, he was a heady rider, but he was also superstitious, and never raced without his good luck charm—a venerable, beaten-up old saddle.

The first time Ben Jones put this antique on Whirlaway, he asked, "Can't you afford a better saddle?" Woolf answered, "I wouldn't swap that saddle for your horse." When Jones reminded Woolf that Whirlaway had won close to half a million dollars, the jockey smiled and said, "That saddle has won more than a million!"

By now, Whirlaway was acknowledged to be king of the handicap division, and the 130 pounds assigned to him for the Arlington Handicap on August 1 proved it. Carrying a staggering weight, ten pounds over his nearest rival, he finished second but came out of it more tired than after any other race. Ben Jones passed up Saratoga to give the colt a rest.

Rhode Island and the Narragansett Special at a mile and three-sixteenths beckoned. The champion, as in the previous year at Santa Anita, arrived in regal splendor, accompanied by his white pony stable companion, his exercise boy, Pinky Brown, and his groom, Dan Barnett. A special stall had been readied for him, and Ben Jones, leading Whirlaway by his halter, let him look around before putting him to bed.

Interest in the race was enormous. Alsab, a Cinderella horse one year Whirly's junior, was to compete. Owned by Al Sabath of Chicago, he had been bought at Saratoga for a mere $700. By the end of his three-year-old year, he had won twenty-one races and almost $300,000.

A match between Alsab and Whirlaway was a natural, but Sabath was difficult and, after a series of on-again, off-again telephone calls, withdrew his colt.

The Narragansett Special was run without Alsab, and Mr. Longtail, with George Woolf up, had no problem in winning the race. Whirlaway was well into the stretch, and more than one-hundred feet behind the leader when he made his move. The long golden tail streamed behind the small chestnut colt as he flew down the track, with "The Iceman" sitting cool and easy in the saddle. Whirlaway put away the other six horses and $24,300; now, with $491,136 in the bank, he was on the threshold of Warren Wright's half-million-dollar dream.

The pressure kept up for a match race between Alsab and Whirlaway. They were both fast horses who had been heavily raced—Alsab with thirty-eight starts in less than two seasons, and Whirlaway with eleven additional races in almost three years. But that was about all they had in common.

Whirlaway, the world's biggest money winner, was impeccably bred with the bluest of the blueblood. *Blenheim II, his sire, had cost $250,000 and Whirlaway had been raised on Calumet's luxurious acres. Trained by the greatest trainer in the country, Ben Jones, Whirlaway was raced heavily, but not over-raced.

Alsab, of nondescript breeding by a stallion called Good Goods, was run off his feet for purses and glory. Basically unsound, he was kept patched together; only his thoroughbred heart kept him going.

On September 19, 1942, the two horses met in a special match race, the Narragansett Championship, one and three-sixteenths miles for $25,000, winner take all. Since this was a weight-for-age race, the elder Whirlaway carried an additional seven pounds.

Both horses liked to come from behind and the early pace was slow. Carroll Bierman was on the rail with Alsab, while George Woolf held Whirlaway two lengths behind all the way to the last turn. Whirlaway started his move and slowly gained on Alsab. The last furlong was head-and-head, with Alsab a nose in front under the wire, although Whirlaway led a few strides past the finish.

The stage was set for another meeting between Alsab and Whirlaway in the two-mile Jockey Club Gold Cup and, since it was weight-for-age, Whirlaway carried 124 pounds to Alsab's 117. Neither horse wanted to go to the front. They all lay behind the leader, The Rhymer, until the half-mile pole where Alsab opened up a lead over Whirlaway. George Woolf waited, and in the last furlong made his run. Whirly finished three quarters of a length ahead of the Sabath colt. He had also broken the half-million-dollar barrier, for the Jockey Club Gold Cup put his winnings at $511,486.

The Pimlico Special was a walkover in the real sense of the

word—a race with only one horse entered. Ten prospective entrants had been invited, but all were frightened off by Mr. Longtail, including Alsab. Two days before, Al Sabath had opted for another race. Whirlaway made a ceremonial entrance and breezed around the course in solitary grandeur, earning $10,000.

He raced three more times and finished his twenty-second and last race of the year, with a record of twelve wins, eight seconds, and two thirds.

For the third year, Whirlaway was the head of his division and, for the second time, he was Horse of the Year. The two-year-old champion was Count Fleet, who was destined to wear the Triple Crown in the next year, 1943.

At the end of the season, Ben Jones announced that Whirlaway would be retired, and he should have been. He had won his half-million dollars and earned a rest, but the temptation to race him was too great and, as the 1943 season began, Whirlaway was again in training.

"If Whirlaway was my horse he would still be running when he was ten years old. He is the soundest horse I've ever seen," said Ben Jones, but even he was not infallible. Whirlaway was raced two times as a five year old, coming in third and fifth, and then pulled up lame. At last Warren Wright decided that the time had come to retire the iron horse. Wright told Whirly's fans, "We feel he is entitled to this and believe he has made a great contribution to racing."

So the racing sun set on this great son of *Blenheim II, whose devastating stretch run in winning the English Derby foretold the dazzling style of Whirlaway.

In five years of racing, he had won a total of $561,161: with thirty-two firsts, fifteen seconds, nine thirds, and was unplaced only four times—a tremendous record.

Scaring off ten prospective entrants, Whirlaway and jockey George Woolf won a one-horse race: the 1942 Pimlico Special.

RACING RECORD

Year	Age	Starts	1st	2nd	3rd	Earnings
1940	2	16	7	2	4	$ 77,275
1941	3	20	13	5	2	272,386
1942	4	22	12	8	2	211,250
1943	5	2	0	0	1	250
	Totals	60	32	15	9	$561,161

Whirly came home a hero. The city of Lexington dubbed August 8, 1943, "Whirlaway Day." There were carrots and sugar for Whirly and speeches for the five thousand people who came to Calumet. Don Ameche, of movie fame, paid his respects, the great colt's praises were sung over nationwide radio, and Mr. Wright was presented with a scroll to take the place of the bronze plaque which was unavailable in wartime.

Mr. Longtail spent the next seven years in the palatial stallion barn at Calumet. He was in great demand as a sire, and through 1951 his American sons and daughters earned well over a million and a half dollars.

In 1950 Whirlaway was seen at Calumet by Marcel Boussac, France's most successful owner. With true Gallic enthusiasm he said, "C'est pour moi," and arranged to lease Whirlaway for three years. Mr. Longtail left Lexington for France, never to return to the Kentucky bluegrass of his birth.

Boussac was France's Warren Wright and his two stud farms, in Normandy and near Paris, were as imposing and immaculate as Calumet.

Whirly enjoyed his work and never looked better. Maybe the famous French cuisine, extended to preparing oats and hay, had turned our Southern boy into a gourmet.

Two years after Whirlaway's arrival in France, Boussac was so pleased that he decided to buy the horse outright. Unfortunately, the following year Whirlaway, the temperamentally difficult but brilliant chestnut, died. He was buried in France, but a headstone bearing his name has a place of honor in the graveyard at Calumet.

COUNT FLEET (1940–1973)	*REIGH COUNT, 1925*	**Sunreigh*
		**Contessina*
	QUICKLY, 1930	*Haste*
		Stephanie

7
Count Fleet
The Fleetest of the Fleet

Count Fleet was a perfect name for the small brown colt by Reigh Count out of Quickly. He ran the fastest mile ever run by a two year old, 1:34⅘, and was owned by John D. Hertz of Hertz Rent-a-Car fame. He never measured more than 15:2 hands, his conformation was uninspiring, and his disposition left much to be desired. But his fantastic running ability caused him to be the first colt seriously considered as an equal to Man o'War.

Count Fleet's trophies and records list his owner as Mrs. John D. Hertz—a gallant gesture by a devoted husband. The real power behind Stoner Creek Stud, where "The Count," as he was known to his fans, was foaled, trained, and died, was John D. Hertz, who turned a hobby into one of the most successful racing stables in the United States.

When young Hertz, aged five, came to Chicago from Ruttka, Czechoslovakia, in 1884, his chance of ever owning anything as luxurious as a horse—even a work horse—was most unlikely. Life was hard for the immigrant boy and, at the age of ten, he ran away from home. Some accounts say that his first job was as an assistant driver for a newspaper delivery wagon, others insist his initial contact with the news media was as an office boy, but all agree that in time he became a sports reporter who covered boxing and racing. He learned to box himself and became an amateur fighter. The old Roby track in Indiana was his introduction to racing, not so much as a reporter, but as a volunteer valet, taking care of the jockeys' muddy clothes and tack.

In 1915, Hertz started to make his fortune as owner of the Yellow Cab Company. Later, his racing colors were to be a solid canary yellow. Mr. Hertz went on to found Hertz Rent-a-Car, which was to become the mammoth, world-wide, car and truck rental agency. He also invested in bus lines, aircraft, movies, and oil. In later years he sold his vast holdings, accepted a partnership in Lehman Brothers, the Wall Street bankers, and devoted more of his time to racing. In both World Wars he was a special advisor on transportation to the Secretary of War.

In 1921, at the suggestion of Roy Carruthers, a friend from his Roby track days, Hertz bought an interest in a racing stable and two years later, in England, he purchased La Dauphine, who became the dam of the stable's first successful runner, Anita Peabody. The Hertzes decided to breed yearlings for the sales at Saratoga, and that was Anita Peabody's destination. She was entered in the August sale, sent to Saratoga, and in due course brought into the sales arena. At the last minute, sentiment triumphed. The Hertzes decided that they didn't want to lose her, and bid her in for $11,000. Whether this was great foresight, instinct, or just plain good luck is anybody's guess, but Anita Peabody became the foundation mare of their stud farm.

If Anita Peabody was the foundation mare, Reigh Count was certainly the foundation sire. Bought from Willis Sharpe Kilmer in 1927 for $12,500, Reigh Count appealed to John Hertz because Mr. Hertz always liked a fighter. In a maiden race at Saratoga, Reigh Count had caught Hertz's eye when he bit his opponent on the neck and then went on to win the race.

Reigh Count was not fashionably bred and some say that his sire *Sunreigh and his dam *Contessina (an English import costing well under a thousand dollars) had a love match rather than an arranged mating. Breeding is an inexact science in which one tries to breed the best to the best—and hopes for the best. *Sunreigh and *Contessina were far from the best, and Reigh Count's breeding promised little. Whatever Hertz's reasoning, his choice was a good one. Only ten days after the purchase, Reigh Count came in second to Anita Peabody in the Futurity.

Many owners of large racing establishments try for a lifetime to win the Kentucky Derby and never succeed, but Reigh Count won the 1928 Derby in one of the largest fields ever, twenty-two horses. The Saratoga Cup, the Lawrence Realization, and the Jockey Club Gold Cup were also his for the asking.

The following year, John Hertz sent Reigh Count to England where he won the Coronation Cup and came in second in the Ascot Gold Cup. All in all, he started twenty-seven times, won twelve, and earned $178,170.

That same year, Hertz established himself as a valued friend of racing in this country. Learning that Al Capone, the Chicago gangster and "the Godfather" of the 1920s, was trying to buy Arlington Park, he organized a group of civic-minded, well-heeled sportsmen and bought the track. His old friend Roy Carruthers was made manager, and honest, big-time racing was preserved in Illinois.

Reigh Count was retired to stud in 1930 and for six years stood at the Hertzes' Leona Stock Farm. Later he was moved to A. B. Hancock Sr.'s Claiborne Farm in Paris, Kentucky, where he remained until his owner, at Hancock's suggestion, purchased the Stoner Creek farm, across the creek from Claiborne.

At first Reigh Count was considered a good, but not a great, stallion. His colts were useful horses who developed late and won numerous, but unimportant, races. They were not Stakes or Futurity material. However, they earned enough to put Reigh Count on the twenty-leading-sires list for five successive seasons. By 1940, Reigh Count was no longer in demand as a stud.

In an interview with John D. Hertz, a reporter asked what his plans were for Reigh Count, and Hertz answered that he would breed about four mares a year to him for as long as he lived. To the newsman, Hertz's breeding program sounded more like loyalty to his own than confidence in the stud. In 1940, Count Fleet, one of Reigh Count's first crop of foals at Stoner Creek, changed everything.

Meanwhile, Hertz was developing his Paris, Kentucky, property. It had been neglected; the fences were falling down, the buildings—what there were of them—were in need of repair, and the pastures were full of weeds. Ralph Baird, Hertz's manager, worked to make it one of the outstanding stud farms in Kentucky. The farm had always been called Stoner Creek, after the winding stream which bisects it, and the creek itself received its name from Mike Stoner, who had camped on the property with his friend Daniel Boone.

Stoner Creek was, and still is, a working stud farm. Instead of white board fences which need continuous painting, brown creosoted fencing encloses the fields. The famous bluegrass pastures, which look as green as any other grass to non-Kentuckians, are carefully maintained, and the barns are numerous and workmanlike. However, the entrance drive at Stoner Creek sets it apart from any other farm. Flanked by dozens of pink and white dogwood trees, the ride from the road to the main house and the farm office in mid-April is as beautiful as Japanese cherry blossom time along the Potomac.

Since 1927, Mr. Hertz had been looking for a mare by the stallion Haste to breed to Reigh Count. He thought that the early two-year-old speed of the Haste colts, combined with the staying ability and somewhat late development of Reigh Count's get, would make what in horse lingo is called a good "nick" or cross. When a Haste mare was finally located, she turned out to be a footsore seven-year-old "plater" named Quickly. Her price was a lowly $2,000.

Quickly's pedigree was interesting if not fashionable. She was by Haste, out of Stephanie, who was by *Stefan the Great. On her dam's side she was a granddaughter of *Rock Sand who was also the grandsire of Man o'War. If that was not sufficient recommendation, her ancestry could be traced back to The Tetrarch, the English spotted horse whose speed was legendary.

Bred by Joseph E. Widener at his Elmendorf Farm in Lexington, she was flighty and not particularly good-looking, but Quickly was quick; she set one track record and equaled two others.

Racing for Mr. Widener, and later for other owners, she ran mostly in six-furlong races for small purses, made even smaller by the Depression. She earned $21,530 in eighty-five starts, of which she won thirty-two, came in second fourteen times, and third a total of thirteen times. She never ran in stakes races and, when Mr. Hertz bought her, she was probably delighted to have the opportunity to cool her sore feet in Stoner Creek.

Quickly was in such poor physical shape when she was bred for the first time that the colt had to be destroyed. The next year she was barren, but in 1940 a gangly brown colt was born. He was named Count Fleet.

Our hero wasn't particularly well put together. His long straight pasterns left much to be desired. A horse's pasterns are considered shock absorbers and Don Cameron, Mr. Hertz's trainer, worried whether Count Fleet would be able to stand the strain of training. His disposition was ornery and he did not endear himself to anyone at Stoner Creek. The decision was to sell him. His price tag was a modest $5,000, but Mr. Hertz could find no takers.

The columnist Red Smith, in his 1973 obituary of Count Fleet, quoted Johnny Longden, the jockey now turned successful trainer in California. Longden told Smith that he was riding for the Hertzes when he heard that Count Fleet was to be sold. This time the price had dropped to $4,500—$500 less than the previous year. Longden felt so strongly about Count Fleet's potential that he called Mr. Hertz.

"The colt is dangerous," Hertz told him. "Some day he'll hurt you."

"I'm not afraid of him," Longden said.

"All right, if you're game enough to ride him, I'll keep him."

Johnny Longden rode him throughout his entire career, and

although the colt started slowly as a two year old, Longden would never be sorry that he had persuaded Mr. Hertz to hold on to him.

Count Fleet lost his first two races in the spring of 1942, but won his maiden on June 19 at Aqueduct, his third time out. The charts said that he closed with a rush, and that was to be his permanent style.

In his first stakes race, the East View, he ran second to Gold Shower, but this position was changed in the Wakefield on July 22 when he crossed the finish line first by four lengths with Gold Shower third.

He was rested for a month, then run in several allowance races in preparation for the all-important Belmont Futurity. A few days before the race, he was clocked at an unbelievable 1:08⅕ in a six-furlong workout. In the actual race, the best he could do was to come in third. Some experts felt that the workout had tired him too much, but the more entertaining theory is that Askmenow, the filly who came in second, was in season and "lover-boy" wanted to stay behind rather than in front of her.

The prestigious Champagne Stakes on October 10 at Belmont put Count Fleet on the map. He not only won the mile race by six lengths, but set the track and world record for the distance by a two year old, at 1:34⅘. Twenty Grand had held the record at 1:36.

The no-account yearling had become a sensational two year old. He was a front-runner who broke fast, pinned his ears back, and then took off. He liked to finish well ahead of the field—the longer the distance, the greater the winning margin.

"I never really knew how fast he could run," said Johnny

Longden, his jockey. But it was fast enough to win all his races for the remainder of the year.

The Pimlico Futurity on October 31 was the next big one, and two-year-old Occupation was the horse to beat. Both colts broke fast and fought for the lead, but Count Fleet sped away from Occupation in the stretch and won by five lengths.

Occupation was hurt in the Pimlico Futurity and could not compete with Count Fleet in his final stakes race of the year, the Walden, at a mile and a sixteenth. The rest of the competition was just not good enough, and Count Fleet cantered across the finish line twenty lengths ahead of his nearest rival.

He had had fifteen starts in his two-year-old year, with ten wins, four seconds, and one third to earn a total of $76,245. Although Occupation was the big money winner with $192,355, Count Fleet was named the champion two year old of 1942.

After a restful winter, Count Fleet carried his two-year-old promise into his three-year-old season. He had won his last three races as a two year old, and he was destined to make a clean sweep of the next six.

His first race in 1943 was the St. James Allowance Purse: one mile and seventy yards at Jamaica on April 13. Count Fleet splashed home through mud and slop to win by an easy three lengths. Heavy going did not phase him. He handled it well and almost seemed to enjoy it.

Only four days later, in the one-and-one-sixteenth-mile Wood Memorial, Count Fleet showed his toughness as well as his speed. He broke well, but was bumped by Vincentive, causing Count Fleet to cut his left hind coronet, just above the hoof. Bleeding hard, he tore after the leader, Blue Swords, considered by many to be his closest rival. In less than a quarter of a mile, he had passed Blue Swords and won by four lengths, missing the track record by two fifths of a second. The rest of the field was outclassed.

The 1943 wartime Kentucky Derby came next. This sixty-ninth running was called the Streetcar Derby; gas was rationed and private vehicles were frowned upon. There was talk of canceling the race, but Matt Winn, manager of Churchill Downs, said that he would hold the Derby even if there were only two horses on the track and two people in the stands.

It would take an act of Congress to keep a Kentuckian away from the Derby. Every means of transportation was used, from the streetcar to the bicycle, and some fans even walked. For once, visitors were in the minority, and Kentuckians had a

A born front-runner, Count Fleet broke fast, pinned his ears back, and then took off.

chance to enjoy their own race in comfort. Mint juleps and hot dogs were available without the peacetime wait.

The famous white twin spires, freshly painted, gleamed, but in the backfield some of the barns had missed their annual refurbishing. Normally a crew of painters worked the year around, using five thousand gallons of paint, to keep Churchill Downs beautiful. In wartime, this mammoth job had to be curtailed. With a gardening staff severely reduced by the draft, the management still set out sixty thousand plants in sixty flower beds, filled one hundred urns with a riot of blooms, and the floral display at Churchill Downs was as beautiful as ever.

Although the attendance was sparse, the entries were adequate—ten colts. After Calumet Farm's Ocean Wave, winner of the Blue Grass Stakes and the Derby Trial, was scratched three hours before the race, only Blue Swords was expected to give The Count competition. Count Fleet led all the way, and again beat Blue Swords by three lengths.

For the spectators it was a dull Derby. The favorite won, the second favorite came in second, and no records were broken, but for the Hertzes it was a great day. Their Reigh Count had won the Derby in 1928, and now his son had done the same fifteen years later.

Bill Corum, the noted reporter who became president of Churchill Downs, said, "Count Fleet could have won pulling a horsecar." Bob Considine put it another way. "The Count is the most dominating three year old since War Admiral."

One week later, a four-horse field was all that the mile and three-sixteenths Preakness could muster, and the odds were a ridiculous fifteen cents on the dollar, the shortest odds ever given in the Preakness. Count Fleet broke in front as usual and stayed ahead throughout the race. No one was able to challenge him, not even Blue Swords, who crossed the finish line eight lengths behind Count Fleet, second once more, like the proverbial bridesmaid who was never a bride.

Next came the one-mile Withers at Belmont Park on May 22. Only two horses challenged The Count in this race, run over the same course as the Champagne Stakes; a year before, Count Fleet's time in the Champagne had set a world record for two year olds. On Withers day the track was muddy. The Count enjoyed himself, but he set no records as he galloped home five lengths in front of his nearest rival, Slide Rule. Blue Swords, tired of being an also-ran, was not entered. Winning the race made Count Fleet the first horse since Sir Barton, in 1919, to win the Derby, the Preakness, and the Withers.

The Belmont Stakes, two weeks later, was also to be a three-horse race. Odds were set at one to twenty, paying five cents on the dollar. The footing was perfect, and rumor had it that Longden was going to let the colt run. Twenty thousand spectators sat on the edge of their seats, glasses glued to their eyes, watching The Count live up to his name by setting a new Belmont record of 2:28$\frac{1}{5}$ for the mile and a half.

According to one unofficial account of the race, Johnny Longden, looking for a record, began to ride Count Fleet hard at the quarter pole, although he knew he had the race won. Count Fleet rewarded him with a fantastic burst of speed, only to shorten stride suddenly and falter. Longden, slowed-up, still crossed the wire an unheard of twenty-five lengths ahead of his nearest rival. Count Fleet had captured the Triple Crown by a total of thirty-six lengths, convincing proof that he was truly the fleetest of the fleet.

He was never to race again. Whether the final burst of speed caused the injury, nobody was willing to say. Although Count

Fleet and Johnny Longden walked proudly into the winner's circle for the presentation ceremony, it was to be their last public appearance together; the colt cooled out lame. At first the injury to his right front ankle did not appear serious, but as the summer passed, it became obvious that retirement was near.

In a shade over twelve months, Count Fleet had raced twenty-one times, won sixteen, and earned a total of $250,300. He had made a clean sweep of his last nine races, winning the Derby, the Preakness, and the Belmont, and had become the sixth Triple Crown winner in United States racing history.

RACING RECORD

Year	Age	Starts	1st	2nd	3rd	Earnings
1942	2	15	10	4	1	$ 76,245
1943	3	6	6	0	0	174,055
	Totals	21	16	4	1	$250,300

At the end of the year he was given the final accolade that United States racing can give a colt; he was named champion three year old and Horse of the Year for 1943. The poll conducted by the Daily Racing Form was unanimous. Unlike so many other great race horses, his career was far from over, and for the next twenty years he dominated racing from his breeding shed at Stoner Creek Stud.

Count Fleet was fortunate in both his trainer and jockey, Don Cameron and Johnny Longden. Had it not been for their patience and understanding, the nervous, high-strung, but brilliant, colt might never have seen Churchill Downs.

Don Cameron came to work for the Hertzes in 1939. He was a big quiet-spoken Californian who had been a track star at college and a balloon pilot during World War I.

His family had long been associated with thoroughbreds, and Don had worked for many prominent owners. However, the long-legged brown colt, born at Stoner Creek in 1940, was the best horse he had ever trained. Considering that there have been only nine Triple Crown winners since 1919, this is not damning Cameron or Count Fleet with faint praise.

Johnny Longden was another tremendous plus in Count Fleet's good fortune. The English-born, Canadian-reared, four-foot-ten-inch jockey was one of the all-time greats. Starting as a stable boy, he became an exercise rider and finally a full-fledged jockey. By the time he retired, Johnny Longden had won 6,026 races and his mounts had earned well over $20 million in purses.

In 1970 Willie Shoemaker won his 6,027th race and broke Longden's record. After congratulating him, Longden, never one to underrate himself, told the assembled group of well-wishers, "It took a good man to set that record, and it took a damn good man to break it."

Like so many other self-made men, Longden thoroughly enjoyed the trappings of wealth and fame—a large Cadillac, an equally impressive diamond ring, and his bust in bronze at Santa Anita Race Track.

Longden was leading United States jockey in 1938, 1947, and 1948, and after his retirement he became a successful trainer in California. Johnny holds the distinction of being the only man who has both ridden and trained a Kentucky Derby winner: Count Fleet in 1943 and Majestic Prince in 1969.

In his long career he rode thousands of horses, but he

considers Count Fleet the greatest, although not the easiest to ride. The Count was hard to rate, impetuous, awkward at the turns, and sometimes uncontrollable. He always ran in blinkers, and occasionally gave the impression that he would rather crash through a fence than bend around it. But all was forgiven when he turned on the speed and annihilated the opposition.

Longden and Mr. Hertz had a most happy relationship; it was almost a mutual admiration society. After winning the Derby, Longden said, full of boyish enthusiasm, "Gee, it sure is fun to ride for you, Mr. Hertz!" When they lost, Hertz would tell him, "Buck up, Johnny. Think of all the races you've stolen for me out there."

While Johnny Longden continued his winning ways on the track, Count Fleet returned to his birthplace, Stoner Creek Stud, in Paris, Kentucky. In the spring of 1944, his first season at stud, his harem consisted of thirty mares, ten owned by the Hertzes and twenty by outsiders. For the rest of the year, he romped in his paddock or dozed in his new private fireproof stallion barn. Built like a small white-painted chapel, complete with slate-gray roof and cupola, it was the height of equine luxury. Deservedly so, for soon the king of the turf would become the leading thoroughbred sire in the United States.

In 1947, Count Fleet's first crop of youngsters came pounding down the track and, a few years later in 1951, the Derby was won by his son, Count Turf. Owned by restaurateur Jack Amiel, who had started by peddling candy in the street, Count Turf was out of Delmarie, a well-bred mare.

His racing record was mediocre, with one win in a stakes race as a two year old and a victory in a six-furlong sprint at three. He was considered Derby material only by his owner, and not by either his trainer, Sol Rutchick, or the public. When Amiel insisted on entering Count Turf in the Derby, Rutchick refused to accompany the colt to Churchill Downs.

Amiel hired an old trainer to meet the license requirements and retained Conn McCreary, considered by many a has-been, as a jockey. The ex-candy peddler and the has-been jockey then trained Count Turf to win the Derby by four impressive lengths.

Reigh Count's family now had three generations of Derby winners: Reigh Count in 1928, Count Fleet in 1943, and Count Turf in 1951. To commemorate the three-generation win, the Hertzes presented a set of racing plates belonging to each of the three Counts to the National Museum of Racing at Saratoga.

That same year, Count Fleet headed the leading sire list. To date, only one other Triple Crown winner, War Admiral, has held this signal honor. Whether Secretariat will join them remains to be seen.

In 1952 another son, One Count, won the Belmont. Count Fleet's fillies not only won races, but produced superhorses. The invincible Kelso, greatest money winner of all time, is out of Maid of Flight, a daughter of Count Fleet. Other good horses out of Count Fleet mares are Lamb Chop, Noble Jay, Prince John, and Fleet Nasrullah.

Ralph Baird, the stud manager who had helped the Hertzes make a showplace of Stoner Creek, retired in 1954. Charles (Charlie, to his friends) Kenney, a most knowledgeable horseman, took over the breeding operation.

The 1963 top broodmare sire award was Count Fleet's, with the offspring of his mares earning $1,866,809, and for the next decade he continued to stand high on the sire list.

The Hertzes and their staff must have been doing something right for, in twenty-four years, Stoner Creek Stud could boast of having raised forty-nine stakes winners, including twelve $100,000 winners and a Triple Crown victor.

The years went by. Both Mr. and Mrs. Hertz died; and in 1964, Stoner Creek was sold to Norman Woolworth and David Johnston, who were interested in raising standardbred horses. Charlie Kenney, now a senior citizen of the horse world, remained as manager, and Count Fleet was promised a home for life.

The Count was officially pensioned in 1965, but the old gentleman did not take kindly to retirement, and in 1967, aged twenty-seven, he had two foals. He also had a new neighbor in his two-stall equine palace. The horse was Nevele Pride, the king of the standardbreds, who had been syndicated for $3 million, an unheard of price in standardbred ranks.

According to Charlie Kenney, The Count was always a loner—polite, but aloof. He never cared for company, human or equine, and a standardbred certainly did not impress him. Nevele Pride, however, paid court to the Triple Crown king. If The Count ambled to the far end of the adjoining paddock, the great standardbred would follow, and if the old horse was moved for any reason, Nevele Pride refused to eat.

The Count still received fan mail, especially Christmas cards. Visitors came to see him but, like most oldsters, he ate, slept, and dreamed his life away. He had one idiosyncrasy. Mr. Hertz had always insisted on having The Count put in his stall in the evening, although many horses are stabled during hot days and turned out in the cool of the night. An old horse, like an old dog, won't learn new tricks, and if Count Fleet was left out, he'd fret and holler. Like a little kid afraid of the dark,

Count Fleet insisted on being tucked into his warm cozy bed at night.

On May 3, 1973, in honor of the thirtieth anniversary of Count Fleet's Derby win, Billy Reed, a Louisville *Courier-Journal* staff writer, paid a visit to The Count. He reported that Count Fleet had all his teeth, his color was still a rich dark brown, and he could still run a little. Quoting Ben Whalen, Count Fleet's groom for the last fourteen years, he wrote, "Shoot, one day last week he (Count Fleet) ran like a two year old . . . there were bones poppin' and crackin', but when he got straightened out, why, you shoulda seen him go!"

Count Fleet had more than lived up to his name and, although he was not a very big horse, he became a giant in the eyes of the racing world. He died peacefully on December 3, 1973, and was buried under the pink and white dogwood trees of Stoner Creek. With the burden and the glory of being the only living Triple Crown winner turned over to Secretariat, Count Fleet could finally go to his rest.

ASSAULT
(1943–1971)

ASSAULT (1943–1971)	*BOLD VENTURE, 1933*	**St. Germans*
		Possible
	IGUAL, 1937	*Equipoise*
		Incandescent

8

Assault

The Clubfooted Comet

The eyes of Texas were upon Assault in 1946 when he became the first Texan horse to win the Triple Crown. Bred and owned by the King Ranch of Kingsville, Texas, and under the tutelage of Max Hirsch, a Texan, he invaded the East to beat the best. Flags flew on all state office buildings in Texas after Assault won the Belmont and thus became the seventh Triple Crown winner in United States racing history. A holiday in his honor was contemplated, but when it was realized that it would be called "Assault Day," the idea was quietly dropped. A new sign with "Assault Slept Here," painted in bold letters, was hung over his stable door.

"Everything is bigger and better in Texas" was only partially true of Assault. He was foaled at the 800,000-acre King Ranch, larger than the state of Rhode Island, but Assault was neither big nor beautiful. He was the nondescript foal of a well-bred but sickly mare named Igual, whose grandam was a full sister to Man o'War. Igual was in such poor shape that she was slated to be destroyed, when Dr. J. K. "Doc" Northway, the ranch's chief veterinarian, discovered an abscess under her stifle. Once it had been opened and drained, the mare improved, but she was never raced. Her first two foals were disappointments, and Assault's appearance promised no miracles.

Assault was by the great King Ranch stallion Bold Venture, who had won two legs of the Triple Crown in 1936. Plain and small, the colt never grew larger than 15:1½ hands and weighed under 1,000 pounds. But he had what every great runner needs, "depth through the heart"—a deep chest with plenty of room for lungs and heart. The white snip on his forehead gave him personality, and the white sock on his near hind leg made him easy to identify.

His family appeared to be jinxed. His dam, Igual, never reached the track, and his full brother, Air Lift, a promising youngster whom Hirsch called a "helluva horse," broke his leg the first time out and had to be destroyed.

Assault barely escaped a similar fate. While still a weanling grazing with his dam, he stepped on a surveyor's stake and drove it through his right forefoot. Texas pasture, even King Ranch style, is not Kentucky bluegrass, but the same accident could have happened in Lexington, or anywhere.

The severe injury had the best of care from Doc Northway. In addition to tending to the thoroughbreds, Dr. Northway had to worry about two thousand breeding and working quarter horses, plus 80,000 dark red Santa Gertrudis cattle, a breed founded by the King Ranch.

For weeks the scrawny colt was nursed in the white stable complex, the nerve center of the ranch veterinary office. Assault's recovery was slow, and even when his foot had healed it was permanently deformed. In time he was turned out in a series of small paddocks. Perhaps he watched the other colts gambol and wondered why he could not buck and play. Perhaps he looked across to the ranch's white-fenced sales corral where, every October, prize Santa Gertrudis cattle and King Ranch quarter horses were sold at auction.

Slowly his foot mended, until one morning Doc Northway graduated him to pasture with the other colts. Wanting to play, he stumbled after them. He had to learn to use his deformed foot, and for the rest of his life he was to be gimpy at the walk and trot, but sound at the gallop.

Soon a racing saddle was placed on his back, a soft rubber snaffle was put into his mouth, and Pastel Garcia, a young Mexican boy, climbed on his back. Pastel ("Pie" in English) was to become his exercise boy and constant companion at the ranch, and in later years often accompanied him on his victorious trips to the East and West coasts. Today Garcia, a little heavier and graying at the temples, is a stable foreman, supervising yearlings and exercise boys at the ranch.

Pie's charge was amenable to training, and he did not object to being ridden. But the bit in his tender mouth bothered him. He fussed with his head at a walk, a habit that was to remain with him for the rest of his life.

Assault joined the other yearlings, and Pie rode him over the wintry fields yellowed by the frost to the mile-long exercise track. Sometimes the colts jigged, sometimes they bucked, often they stood straight up in the air. But exercise boys on yearlings anticipate trouble. They do not ride with stirrups quite as short as jockeys and often, before a bucking exhibition takes place, they drop their feet out of the irons to have more grip on the horse.

Cowhands heading for the range, their faces leatherlike from sun and wind, would stop their hardworking quarter horses to watch the antics of the fancy thoroughbreds that their boss, "Mr. Bob," (owner Robert Kleberg, Jr.) had brought to the ranch. What good was a lightheaded youngster who could run, but could not neck-rein or cut a calf out of a herd? Chewing tobacco, they shook their stained sombreros and rode on.

The sand track, as carefully manicured as any big-time racecourse and surrounded by evergreen cedars, was the youngsters' proving ground. The course stretched ahead of them, white-fenced with chocolate-brown trim, the ranch's racing colors. The colts first walked through the starting gate, that mechanical monster which often caused so much trouble. Assault stumbled as they jogged to the quarter pole, a habit which continued long after his foot stopped hurting. At the half-mile pole the youngsters broke into a canter and the chestnut colt's stride became rhythmical. No one was asked for speed at this stage, but as the yearlings breezed past the viewing stand they looked less like gangly babies and more like the racers they were to become. "His stumbling dumped me plenty," said Pastel Garcia, "but he ran so good that I didn't care."

The weeks turned into months and soon after his second birthday, on January 1, 1945, Assault and the other King Ranch two year olds were sent on a long train-ride to Columbia, South Carolina, the winter quarters of Max Hirsch, the King Ranch's legendary trainer. As they chugged eastward, four colts to a boxcar, bedded knee-deep in straw, it seemed like a miracle that the crippled colt, Assault, had come this far and was considered sound enough to be put into serious training.

Max Hirsch had no great expectations for the chestnut colt, but in a racing enterprise as large as the King Ranch, one more horse in training made little difference. There were many promising two year olds. Some, like Halley's Comet, caused great initial excitement, only to fade and disappear in their all-important three-year-old year.

Assault was fortunate to find himself in the barn of Max Hirsch, the superb talent scout who had discovered horses like Grey Lag, Bold Venture, Middleground, and High Gun, as well as many young jockeys, among them Ira Hanford and Bill Boland.

Born in Fredericksburg, Texas, Hirsch started racing quarter horses at the Morris Ranch when he was only ten. He graduated to the thoroughbreds owned by this venerable family, whose racing colors, registered with The Jockey Club, are the oldest in the United States.

In 1893, aged twelve, he disregarded Horace Greeley's "Go West, young man" and hopped a freight going East with a load of Morris horses. Dressed in warm-weather Texas clothes, he arrived cold, hungry, and unsure that he had made the right decision. Wyndham Walden, director of the Morris racing activities, took charge. Hirsch became an exercise boy and rode his first race at fourteen.

He had 123 winners in 1,117 races, but when he grew too big to be a jockey, he took out a trainer's license. Over the years, until his death at eighty-nine, he established a reputation as one of the all-time greats of the racing game.

Hirsch, a widower for many years, ran a well-staffed training stable and home. A dapper dresser who appreciated the good life, he enjoyed the company of the racing fraternity, who dined with him in his cottages at Belmont, Saratoga, and Columbia, South Carolina.

The talents of Virgie, his longtime cook, were appreciated

by all, including Assault. She loved baking and would often make a cake for a winner. Later on, Assault had his share; chocolate was his favorite, icing and all.

Hirsch always ran a public stable, and one of his biggest clients was Morton L. Schwartz. Hard hit by the depression, Schwartz sold out in 1934, and Max Hirsch supervised the dispersal of the racing string.

In the early thirties, the income from oil and natural gas wells on the King Ranch enabled Robert Kleberg, Jr. to enter into racing with a flourish. On Hirsch's advice, he bought Schwartz's Bold Venture as well as a number of good broodmares.

In 1936 Hirsch became the King Ranch trainer, and in that same year Bold Venture won the Derby and the Preakness. It was a fortunate purchase on another count, for his progeny accounted for much of the ranch's future racing success.

Assault, Bold Venture's son, was a good-natured colt, full of nervous energy, but never mean. He continued to stumble badly enough at a walk and trot to throw his rider, and shoeing him was a major operation. The wall of his injured foot was so brittle that a special shoe had to be designed. It was always a case of trial and error. If the shoe stayed on, and the colt galloped well, it was a success, but if the shoe came off, and Assault left the track lame, John Dern, the blacksmith, would try again. Dern became Assault's personal blacksmith and in later years, like a Broadway star's dresser, traveled all over the country with him.

That first winter in Columbia, under the watchful eye of Max Hirsch, the colt learned to handle his deformed foot, to pace himself, and to run. He became part of the gang. Early every morning the youngsters were worked in sets of three or four on the training track. The soil was sandy and good for their feet; the slash and loblolly pine provided a green fragrance, and the mild winter sun warmed the stable area. It was an ideal spot for race horses to learn their trade, to grow and to dream of future conquests.

In April the stable moved to Belmont Park. Stable Number One was Max's barn. Buckets and feed tubs were painted in the King Ranch brown and white. The famous Running W—a brand possibly dating back to the Spaniards who first settled the part of southern Texas that became the King Ranch—was on all equipment. Dogs, cats, and even chickens shared the stable area. Nervous thoroughbreds enjoy companionship, and Max Hirsch okayed the Noah's Ark-like invasion. The mutt, Homely, became Assault's constant companion. Many years later when Homely died, Mrs. Tad Legere, Hirsch's assistant for thirty years, lamented, "Homely was half Labrador and half of my heart."

Now the serious work began. The morning gallops became longer and faster. Assault grew increasingly fit and wanted to run. On June 12 he entered his first race.

"Why run a horse with a foot like that?" a railbird was heard to say as the chestnut came out on the track. Perhaps his critic was right, Assault came in an uninspiring twelfth. He ran almost weekly in small purse races, improving each time out. And on July 12, 1945, at Aqueduct, he broke his maiden, winning his first race by a length and a quarter, for $1,915.

"He never showed any sign that it hurt him," Hirsch said, referring to Assault's deformed hoof. "When he walked or trotted you'd think he was going to fall down, but he galloped true. There wasn't a thing wrong with his action when he went fast."

Hirsch, noted for discovering young unknowns, felt that Assault showed promise, but the racing public had little faith and registered their disdain by sending him off at an insulting 71–1 in The Flash, his second stakes race. The Flash, usually run at Saratoga, was held at Belmont that year due to the war. Max bet a packet and Assault did not fail him. He won by a nose and brought home $11,505 in prize money. He ended his two-year-old year having won two out of nine starts and richer by $17,250.

The all-important third year, 1946, started in April for Assault. Max Hirsch attempted to ready the colt for the Kentucky Derby, although he disliked this race and felt that it was too long a course for so early in the season. For the same reason, the great Man o'War was never a contender in the Derby.

Assault's first outing was in the six-furlong Experimental Handicap at Jamaica on April 9. A winner by four and a half lengths, he then went on to cross the finish line first in the somewhat longer Wood Memorial. Shipped to Churchill Downs, he flubbed the Derby Trial on April 30. "*I* lost the race, not Assault," was Hirsch's comment. He had equipped the horse with boots which, on the muddy track, had accumulated enough weight to slow down any thoroughbred, let alone the "Clubfooted Comet."

On May 4 he entered the Kentucky Derby, not as the favorite, but at a mediocre 8–1. It was the first $100,000-added Kentucky Derby. Warren Mehrtens, Max Hirsch's contract jockey, was in the saddle as the band struck up "My Old Kentucky Home" and the horses came out on the track. "Assault was always a curious colt, wanting to stop and look at the sights," Warren Mehrtens recalled. "He wasn't spooky, and if you let him look, he was never any trouble, but if you tried to hustle him, he could get rank."

The seventeen-horse field got off to a good start, Spy Song took the lead, but on entering the stretch, Assault came through on the inside, swept past the tiring pacesetter, and crossed the finish line eight decisive lengths ahead of Spy Song. The traditional blanket of roses was undisputedly his.

Nowadays a horse is given a two-week breather between the Derby and the Preakness, but in 1946 these two important races were held only one week apart.

The day after the Derby the chestnut colt was shipped to Pimlico, and there Joseph Dern, his blacksmith, and Yank, his groom, tended his ever troublesome foot. A smart horse, Assault always tried to take the weight off his tender hoof. He enjoyed resting with this foot immersed in a tub of ice; Yank, his groom, was the iceman, and Assault thrived under his care.

After his Derby victory, the public made him the Preakness favorite. He upheld their faith, but only by a nose. Hirsch had schooled the colt to come from behind. Overanxious, young Mehrtens asked him to move too soon, and Lord Boswell challenged his lead. Assault just managed to stick his nose under the wire first in a grueling finish. $96,620 and a blanket of black-eyed susans were his hard-earned reward.

The Belmont—the race in which his sire had not been entered in 1936—came two weeks later. Perhaps, because of his near-miss in the Preakness, Assault was not the betting favorite in the seven-horse race. The public was not altogether wrong. Assault stumbled badly at the start, almost unseating his rider. "Mr. Hirsch made us ride longer than most," Warren Mehrtens explained. "If it hadn't been for that, I would have been a goner." Mehrtens managed to make a quick recovery and placed the colt on the inside in the mile and a half race. Coming to the outside at the head of the stretch, he drew away from Natchez, his nearest rival, and won the third leg of the Triple Crown by three lengths.

Assault's victory made him $75,400 richer. Virgie, Hirsch's cook, baked a brown and white cake in the ranch colors and Assault demolished it.

He made it four in a row by winning the mile-and-a-quarter Dwyer Stakes. The handicappers thought that no three year old could beat him. Assault was shipped to Chicago's Arlington Park and came in dead last in the Arlington Classic. Something was very wrong. He was rushed back to his stall in agony; kidney stones was the diagnosis. Assault was rested for six weeks and ran again in early September. He was always in the money, but did not place first again until the Pimlico Special on November 1. Now he was running against older horses, but especially against a horse two years his senior named Stymie.

Stymie was not just any horse. He had been owned by the King Ranch and bred by Assault's trainer Max Hirsch. Because he was dangerous to handle and Mr. Kleberg felt he might kill someone, Stymie had been put in a $1,500 claiming race, and was claimed by a rival trainer, Hirsch Jacobs. When Max had a chance to claim the horse back in a $3,500 race, he passed up the opportunity. "I didn't want to give Jacobs a $2,000 profit!" he said. In later years, when Stymie had won $918,000 and Max was ribbed about his error, the wizard who had trained more than 100 stakes winners philosophized, "It all boils down to foresight never being as good as hindsight."

When Assault and Stymie met on the track, Max Hirsch was hard pressed to prove that Assault was the better horse. He put the veteran jockey, Eddie Arcaro, up on Assault in the

Pimlico Special and told him, "Just wait for Stymie." Arcaro waited and did not turn Assault loose until Stymie got up to his girth. The new strategy worked, and Stymie was beaten by six lengths. Assault was named Horse of the Year, the coveted award given by the *Morning Telegraph.*

His final race for 1946 was the Westchester Handicap at Empire City. He won $38,600 in the Westchester, bringing his total earnings for the year to $424,195. This was some $100,000 more than the purses earned by Gallant Fox, the second Triple Crown winner, and reflected the increase in purse money in the intervening sixteen years.

Assault had had a triumphant season as a three year old, but he performed even better at four in the handicap division. He won five out of seven starts to become the biggest four-year-old money winner of all time.

As 1947 got under way, Whirlaway, the '41 Triple Crown winner, was "Mr. Moneybags" with a lifetime total of $516,161 earned. By July, following the Brooklyn Handicap, his fourth straight victory, Assault had pulled ahead with $576,670. He held the title for two short weeks, only to be surpassed by his arch rival, Stymie, with $595,500. For the rest of the season, *numero uno* ping-ponged between the two equine giants. They so concentrated on each other that little attention was paid to a newcomer, Armed, owned by the Calumet Farm, who was to beat them both.

Handicap races make up the bulk of the quality competitions open to older horses. A good race is a close race and by assigning top weight to the best horse, the handicapper attempts to even out the competition. As a pound of weight is considered equal to one length at the finish of a race a mile or over, the more weight a horse carries, the harder he must run.

In the Grey Lag Handicap in May of 1947, Assault was assigned 128 to Stymie's 126 pounds. Assault beat him by a neck. In the Dixie, Assault's burden increased by a pound and in the Suburban he was asked to carry 130, four pounds more than Stymie. The Clubfooted Comet romped home, leaving Stymie a poor fourth, ten lengths behind. Less than a month later in the Brooklyn, he carried nine pounds more than Stymie and still beat him by three lengths.

The Butler Handicap, the fifth and last race of his winning streak, was considered by many to be his finest hour. Carrying an unbelievable 135 pounds and giving Stymie 9, he crossed the wire leading Stymie by a head. The great Eddie Arcaro, whose orders were to wait for Stymie, was his rider. Arcaro may have waited too long, for, at the crucial moment, Assault was boxed in. Tad Legere, who watched the race from the King Ranch box, recalled, "It almost looked as if Assault decided to take over. He flattened his ears, found a minute opening and forced his way through, beating Stymie by a head."

When Max Hirsch congratulated Arcaro on having ridden a powerful race, Arcaro gave the credit to Assault. "I rode a powerful horse," he told the trainer. After that exhibition, the racing fraternity agreed with Max Hirsch that although Stymie was a great horse, Assault was still greater.

Two years earlier Max Hirsch had marveled that Assault was sound enough to train, and by the middle of the victorious season of 1947, clouds were gathering on Assault's horizon. His foot was as sound as it would ever be, but his legs and general health were causing concern. The will to win was always there, but sometimes all the little horse could run on was heart; his fragile underpinnings were showing hard wear. He should have quit after the Butler Handicap, but he was entered for the Gold Cup one week later, and Stymie beat him.

A match race for $100,000 between Armed and Assault was next on the schedule. Chicago's Arlington Park was the location, and Assault was shipped to the windy city. He did not have Pie Garcia, his regular exercise jockey, for his final workout before the race, and the new boy couldn't ride him well. Assault took off, severely straining himself, and was dead lame when he left the track. The match was postponed and rescheduled for the end of September at Belmont Park.

Assault developed a splint and the race should have been canceled. George Widener, president of The Jockey Club, had arranged for the race; Ben Jones, another superb trainer, wanted to see his Armed beat the champ; and Bob Kleberg, Assault's owner, did not wish to withdraw the horse for the second time. For once, Max Hirsch had nothing to say.

"The race will go on," Mr. Kleberg announced. The Belmont officials permitted no betting on the race. Assault tried his best, but Armed beat him by eight lengths.

That winter Assault raced twice in Florida, winning one race, but his ailments persisted and he was sent to stud. He proved to be sterile, and in the spring of 1949 he was put back to work. He raced six times, and had one good win in the Brooklyn Handicap at Aqueduct. After the New York meeting closed, he was to be sent, via Texas, to California to Buddy Hirsch, Max Hirsch's son, who trained the King Ranch string on the West Coast.

After resting at the King Ranch, Assault was put on a train to Los Angeles. His old friend, Pie Garcia, accompanied him, and a young veterinarian, Monte Moncreif, one of Dr.

Northway's bright young men and today the chief veterinarian, went along to supervise.

The train left the ranch and reached El Paso in a snowstorm. After being assured that it would not depart for at least two hours, Dr. Moncreif left to make a telephone call. "It wasn't a long conversation," he recalled, "but when I got back, the train and Assault had vanished." Today, almost thirty years later, he still pales when he talks about the incident.

Pie was alone in the boxcar with Assault. There was a suitcase of medicines, but no one to administer them. "I couldn't get the boxcar door shut," said Pie recently, "and I was worried about hobos and the cold. I was scared stiff that my horse would get pneumonia, but he got to California OK."

Moncreif, meanwhile, frantically arranged for air transportation out of El Paso. He managed to arrive in Los Angeles well ahead of his charge and was waiting in the yard as the train pulled in. When Pie saw Moncreif, his face lit up like a Mexican sunrise as he shouted, *"Hola, Compa're."*

Assault joined Buddy Hirsch's string at Hollywood Park. He won one small preparatory race, was third in the Westwood Purse, and seventh in the Hollywood Gold Cup, which was his forty-second and last race.

His clubfoot, various splints, a wrenched ankle, and a bad knee have been copiously covered by other writers, but little has been mentioned about the problem that finally forced his retirement in 1950. Assault had become a bleeder, and bled from the nose after any exertion. He was sent back to the ranch and turned out with a bunch of mares. And a debate still goes on about whether he did or did not get some of the quarter horse mares in foal.

RACING RECORD

Year	Age	Starts	1st	2nd	3rd	Earnings
1945	2	9	2	2	1	$ 17,250
1946	3	15	8	2	3	424,195
1947	4	7	5	1	1	181,925
1948	5	2	1	0	0	3,250
1949	6	6	1	1	1	45,900
1950	7	3	1	0	1	2,950
	Totals	42	18	6	7	$675,470

The years were kind to Assault. He was pensioned off near the ranch veterinary complex where his old friend Pie Garcia watched over his every need, and Doc Northway and Monte Moncreif checked up on his every ailment. When necessary, a secretary was added to the staff to answer his sacks of fan mail. Often letters addressed to ASSAULT, TEXAS, were delivered to him. He answered every one of them with his picture.

Assault died of old age at twenty-eight in 1971 and was buried on the ranch. His headstone is of Texas granite, the same stone used in the state capitol. Doc Northway, who had taken care of him his whole life, insisted that he should be laid to rest with his legs in running position and facing west—an old cavalry tradition.

To this day, the walls of the dining room in the main ranch house are covered with three huge blowups of Assault winning the Derby, the Preakness, and the Belmont Stakes.

CITATION
(1945–1970)

	BULL LEA, 1935	**Bull Dog*
		Rose Leaves
	**HYDROPLANE II, 1938*	*Hyperion*
		Toboggan

9
Citation
He Was a Cadillac

WHIRLAWAY PUT CALUMET FARM AND THE JONES BOYS on the racing map, but Citation, almost a decade later, was the superstar in Calumet's Milky Way.

Whirlaway, erratic and very difficult, had flashes of greatness and was the best of his time, but Citation was the greatest of the great—possibly even better than Man o'War or Secretariat. The Calumet Comet had everything—disposition, brains, speed at all distances and under any condition. As Eddie Arcaro said about his favorite horse, "He was a Cadillac; my little daughter Caroline could have ridden him."

In 1947, Citation's first year at the track, the bay colt won $155,680 and was named two year old of the year. In those same twelve months, Calumet had so many other great horses running that the farm banked $1,402,236, the first million-dollar year for any racing stable in the world.

Some called it Calumet luck. Others said, "If it's by Bull Lea from a Blenheim mare by Ben Jones, how could anyone miss?"

Bull Lea, by Bull Dog out of Rose Leaves, was Citation's sire. After winning ten races and $94,825, he lost the 1938 Derby to Lawrin, trained by Ben Jones. A disappointment at the time, it was an example of Calumet luck, for his defeat was the reason for Warren Wright's hiring of Ben Jones.

Bull Lea, a big brown horse with a kindly disposition, fathered great colts—Citation, Hill Gail, Iron Liege, Coaltown, and Ponder, but his fillies became collectors' items as broodmares. Among dozens of good ones, his daughter Two Lea foaled Tim Tam, who almost won the Triple Crown, and another daughter, Bewitch, was leading money-winning mare. Bull Lea was the leading broodmare sire for four years. From him descends much of the cream of American racing. He died in 1964, and his life-like statue in bronze overlooks the peaceful oval graveyard at Calumet.

In the nineteen forties, Warren Wright and the Joneses should have been prosecuted for violating the Sherman Anti-Trust Act; Calumet was a combination in restraint of racing. Milton Menasco, the well-known equine artist, preserved the incriminating evidence in living color. He painted a portrait of the Jones boys, astride their lead ponies, flanking nine horses all ready to run. There were bays, bright chestnuts, and shiny browns, and their names were Citation, Armed, Faultless, Wistful, Bewitch, Fervent, Two Lea, Ponder, and Coaltown. It was like having a football team with nine Joe Namaths.

In this period Calumet had six years with winnings of over $1 million. The bank account grew and so did the trophy room in the main house. When the Joneses arrived at Calumet in 1939, Mr. and Mrs. Wright had a handful of cups; when Jimmy Jones left in 1964, more than 500 trophies covered the shelves of the horseshoe-shaped trophy room, including two three-sided Triple Crown vases and a host of solid gold cups. The collection became so valuable that it began to spend more time in a bank vault in Lexington than in the owner's residence at Calumet Farm.

Citation, the Bull Lea colt out of *Hydroplane II, was a nice-looking horse, but not as handsome as his father, or as flashy as the golden chestnut Whirlaway. He was started as a yearling by Ben Jones. By 1947, Ben was ready to take it a little easier, and the responsibility for the racing operation went, more and more, to his son, Horace Allyn Jones. "Jimmy" had worked alongside his father from Ben's start at Calumet in 1939, and the Jones boys could do no wrong.

Ben Jones considered Citation the most intelligent horse he had ever handled, and that probably accounted for the colt's great adaptability. Citation won sprints and distance races, under different jockeys, at tracks in seven states. He won whether the track was hard, soft, or covered with two inches of clinging mud.

In 1947, his two-year-old year, he was beaten only once—in the Washington Park Futurity. Jimmy Jones said that this was not really a valid defeat, because Calumet had entered three horses—Bewitch, Citation, and Free America—any one of which could have won the race. He had told the jockeys not to overextend their two year olds to beat one other. If they were all in the first three, let whoever was in front keep his position, and the jockeys' share of the winnings would be split three ways. True to Jimmy Jones's prediction, Calumet wrapped up the first three places, with Bewitch ahead of Citation.

This was proper, for in most American races, unlike racing in some European countries, all horses with the same owner and/or trainer are coupled in the betting as an entry, and a victory by any one counts equally in the betting.

Citation's last two-year-old race, and his first race at over a mile, was the Pimlico Futurity at one mile and one-sixteenth. The experts had said that a Bull Lea colt was no good over a distance, but Citation proved them wrong. Under 119 pounds, he finished one and one-half lengths ahead of the King Ranch's Better Self to add $36,675 more to his account.

With the increase in Florida racing, eastern horses no longer took the winter off. They were shipped from New York and Maryland by train to Hialeah. "Sometimes we'd send as many as six boxcars filled with race horses," Jimmy Jones recalled. "We'd attach them to a passenger express, but I'd try to pick one that made a few stops. Otherwise, the horses would be standing up and holding on all the time." It's hard to think of a horse holding on, but just like a standing passenger in a subway car, horses do have to concentrate on keeping their balance.

The horses, four or six to a boxcar and bedded down in deep straw, did not mind the trip, and neither did the men who traveled with them. Citation's groom Dave Barnett, like all the other men, slept with his charge. The track kitchen packed a basket of food, and while the horses were fed and watered, the men, sitting on tack trunks or bales of hay, ate their picnics.

Only the Joneses traveled by Pullman. "On a long haul, whenever the train stopped I'd have the dining car send a hot meal to the men. It was quite a sight seeing half a dozen waiters in white coats parading down the platform, balancing trays of food," Jimmy Jones recalled.

Once the long journey was over, the horses would take about a week to get back into running condition. After balancing for several days and nights in their swaying stalls, they would need to find their land legs. First they were walked for a day or so, then jogged, galloped, and finally breezed in preparation for their next race.

Citation started at Hialeah Park in February in a six-furlong overnight race, the Ground Hog Purse, and had his first win as a three year old. He beat four stakes winners, including his stablemate—1947's Horse of the Year, Armed.

In the Seminole Handicap, open to three year olds and up, Citation took on his elders and won it. In the Everglades Handicap seven days later, Al Snider, his rider, made a move three furlongs from home, and the handsome bay colt imperceptibly shifted gears and crossed the finish line first with his ears pricked. The word was getting around that this was the horse to beat in the Kentucky Derby.

His last race in Florida was the Flamingo Stakes, one and one-eighth miles for three year olds—the Florida equivalent of the Kentucky Derby. Saggy took the lead. This improbably-named colt, owned by Mrs. Stanley Sagner, was by Swing and Sway. Saggy and Pennant Day had Citation boxed behind them on the rail, and the racegoers, who had bet Citation down to 1 to 5, started to get nervous. There was no need to worry; Al Snider let out a notch and zipped between the two horses like a hot knife through butter. When the stop watches were read, Citation had pared three-fifths of a second off the track record and pocketed $43,500 for first place.

At the end of the Hialeah meeting, Al Snider, who had ridden Citation so brilliantly, took a few days off. Snider and two friends were on a fishing cruiser off the Florida keys when they disappeared. The blue Caribbean had claimed three more lives.

With Snider dead, Jimmy Jones called on Eddie Arcaro. Ben Jones had retained "Heady Eddie" to win the Derby with

Lawrin in 1938 and Whirlaway in 1941. Now the old master was getting a third chance with a Jones product.

Ben Jones may still have been masterminding the Calumet operation, but son Jimmy was now officially in charge. Jimmy Jones became head trainer after his father retired, and only left Calumet in 1964 to take over the management of the Monmouth Park race track.

Today, Jimmy Jones sits behind his desk in his handsome office at Monmouth, looking the picture of a round gray-haired cherub. Crowding the walls, the bookshelves, and the desk are pictures and statuettes of his great horses. Of course, Citation, with Eddie Arcaro up, is in the position of honor.

When he has time, Jimmy Jones loves to lean back in his chair and talk about Citation, but this doesn't happen too often. With homes in Missouri, New Jersey, and Florida, Jones flies his own plane and is almost always on the move.

If one can catch up with him when there is no racing at Monmouth Park, he may take time to tell about Eddie Arcaro, who he still thinks was the greatest, and how he could always count on Heady Eddie's good judgment. As an example, he may mention the Chesapeake Trial in 1948. It was Arcaro's first ride on Citation and the colt's only defeat of his three-year-old year.

Once again, Citation was running against Saggy, and an equally improbably-named horse called Hefty, who set the pace over a muddy six furlongs. When Arcaro made a move, Hefty carried Citation so wide that Arcaro could not make up the distance. Thanks to Hefty, Saggy won! Later Arcaro said that he was not about to burn up Citation on a muddy track in a small race, with the big $100,000 stakes coming up.

The Chesapeake Stakes, five days later, was another story.

The racing public discounted the previous week's trial with Hefty and Saggy, and Citation was an overwhelming favorite. Arcaro and Citation quickly disposed of Saggy and won handily.

Churchill Downs and the Derby Trial saw Citation once more in the winner's circle. The stage was now set for Colonel Winn's masterpiece, the Kentucky Derby.

The Derby was, and still is, a happening. Never has a single race owed so much to any individual as the Kentucky Derby owes to Matt Winn. A genius at public relations, Winn took a historic race, which was too early in the season to be popular, and with a shrewd admixture of ballyhoo and good horse sense made it the top race in the United States.

Citation was the overwhelming favorite. But he was coupled with his stablemate Coaltown, a blazing-fast Bull Lea colt out of a *Blenheim II mare. This gave Warren Wright two horses who could win the Derby.

Citation was favored to beat Coaltown, although the records showed that only one winner of the Derby Trial, Black Gold, had ever won the Derby. Coaltown had had a meteoric win in the Blue Grass Stakes at Keeneland just before the Derby, and even Arcaro was doubtful. As Ben Jones hoisted him into Citation's saddle, Arcaro asked, "Are you sure I'm on the right one?" The elder Jones merely nodded and replied, "Eddie, if I thought Coaltown would win this Derby, you would be on him."

It had rained buckets during the previous night and even Ben and Jimmy Jones had doubts. But the only contest was between Coaltown and Citation. Coaltown, with Pierson up, shot out of the gate like a frightened deer and took the lead, with Citation right beside him. Pierson kept the lead, hoping to run the rest of the horses off their feet. Arcaro played it differently and, taking no chance of being boxed in, took the middle path.

Down the backstretch, a half mile from home, Arcaro loosened his hold on the reins slightly and drew up to second place, three lengths behind Coaltown. At the quarter pole Arcaro had Citation alongside his stablemate, and they skimmed through the slop as if tied together. Then the inimitable Arcaro moved his velvet hands a fraction, and the race was over. It was Citation by three and one-half lengths. His first six furlongs, at 1:11⅖, was one fifth of a second faster than Whirlaway's record Derby and the fastest three-quarters of a mile in any Derby since fractional times were first reported in 1903.

Arcaro gave half his winnings to Al Snider's widow, and Mr. Wright matched the sum. A fitting tribute by two gentlemen.

Since man first rode a horse, no one has fully analyzed the ingredients that make a great rider. Split-second timing and judgment, of course, but some riders have an uncanny ability to make themselves one with their mounts. Arcaro was of this rare breed. As Jimmy Jones said of Citation's first three jockeys, "Citation always fought Dodson, went well for Snider, but for Arcaro, Citation ran with a smile on his face."

There was no competition for the Preakness. Ben Jones took Coaltown to New York, while Jimmy went to Pimlico with Citation. Again the betting on Citation was for first only, and it closed with Citation at an unbelievable one to ten.

There were only three other horses entered—C. V. Whitney's Vulcan's Forge, S. W. Labrot's Bovard, and the King Ranch's Better Self—so everyone was to get a piece of the action. After a good start, Citation sprinted under a strong hold and galloped easily in front to the head of the stretch.

Vulcan's Forge tried hard, keeping second position after the first half-mile, but he could do no better than second, by five and one-half lengths in the very heavy going.

Citation had now earned $423,700 and was the sixth, and youngest, of the leading American money winners.

It was four weeks until the Belmont, and Jimmy Jones felt that his colt needed a race in between. He chose the Jersey Stakes at Garden State Park for Citation's workout. The winner by eleven lengths, Citation ran the mile and one-quarter in 2:03, a new track record, and brought home $43,300.

With the Belmont Stakes, the knock-down-the-favorite club was in full cry. "No Bull Lea colt can go a distance. Citation is a good horse but he won't last a mile and a half." Even Jimmy Jones wondered a little. He knew he had a superb colt—but a mile and a half?

There was a field of seven giant-killers out to prove that Citation could be beaten and, for one breathtaking moment, it looked possible. Citation, on the rail, stumbled coming out of the gate, but he quickly recovered and was still in first position. Under a strong hold, Citation stayed in front all the way. Arcaro let him run on for the last half-mile and he later said, "He ran so fast he scared me." The Calumet colt finished eight lengths ahead of the King Ranch's Better Self, whose jockey, Warren Mehrtens, had won the Triple Crown on Assault two years previously. It meant another $77,700 for Calumet.

Like any great athlete, Citation made it look easy. With speed in reserve, he skimmed effortlessly across the finish line, ears pricked forward, seemingly listening for the plaudits of

Citation, the Calumet Comet, took the Derby by three and one-half lengths . . .

the crowd. At 2:28⅕ he had equaled Count Fleet's record, and even the most cynical of the turf writers started using words like "superb" and "as good as Man o'War."

Calumet and Eddie Arcaro had tied William Woodward's Belair Stud. Both stables had won two Triple Crowns: Belair, with Gallant Fox and Omaha, was matched by Calumet's Whirlaway and Citation. It took twenty-five years for Secretariat to win the next Triple Crown, and no other stable has won it twice.

Winning the Derby, the Preakness, and the Belmont made

. . . the Preakness by five and one-half, and the Belmont by eight full lengths.

Citation a superstar, but the level-headed bay did not crave attention. He was all business and didn't even care about tidbits. Oats, hay, water, and a chance to run were what he liked. He was an independent soul, never whinnying for company or palling up with a goat or dog, but he did like his star accommodations.

The Calumet special for their top horses was a series of large screens placed in front of the horses' stalls. Once attached to the stall, the screens formed a locked front porch, bug-and-people proof. Some at the track called it "The Lion Cage."

Joe H. Palmer, the noted sports reporter, wrote at the time: "Several jockeys were discussing Citation last week, and the pleasure it would be to ride him. 'Maybe I could pay Ben Jones to let me ride him around the track in the morning,' one of them hazarded.

" 'You think you could?' asked another. 'You don't know how they take care of that horse. Nobody gets on him in the morning but his regular exercise boy. And do you know how they graze him? They pick out a patch of grass that looks all right, and they let three other horses graze on it a while. Three days later, if they're still all right, they let Citation graze on it.'

"Since possession of Citation was virtually the same as a license to print money, it was quite understandable, if slightly exaggerated."

Citation ran nine more times as a three year old and won every race. He earned $709,470 for the year, giving him a total of $865,150.

He was Horse of the Year, best sprinter, best handicap horse, best three year old; the only goal left was to win $46,185 to pass Stymie, Hirsch Jacobs' great colt who, a few years previously, had become the world's leading money winner.

The most meaningful plaudits were from the handful of great older trainers who had seen them all. Max Hirsch said once again, "There's never been a horse like that." "Sunny Jim" Fitzsimmons, the trainer of Gallant Fox and Omaha, repeated, "Citation's done more . . . than any horse I ever saw—and I saw Man o' War."

On December 14, 1948, Citation developed an inflammation in the fetlock joint.

The treatment was "firing" with a new electric cautery. Its

hot needles made three hundred perforations in the leg, and Citation was shipped to Hialeah to recuperate. He seemed to be making a good recovery, but then there were setbacks. Mr. Wright and the Joneses decided to take him out of racing for an indeterminate period.

The Calumet Comet was given a year off. He ate Kentucky bluegrass and became big and fat. Gradually his leg healed. Perhaps he should have been retired, but two more plateaus were his to climb.

His owner, Warren Wright, became ill in 1949 and never recovered. Wright's widow and Jimmy Jones knew that the old gentleman had set his heart on having Citation beat Stymie's record and go on to become the first equine millionaire.

In 1950 Citation went back to work. After several preparatory sprints, his big race was the Santa Anita Handicap, possibly the greatest winter race in the country. There he met *Noor. In 1948 he could have beaten him, but two years later he was not the Citation of old and *Noor became his nemesis.

*Noor, a son of Nasrullah, had been bred by the Aga Khan and ran third in the Epsom Derby. He was then bought by California's Charles S. Howard, the owner of the legendary Seabiscuit who had won the same race ten years previously.

Citation couldn't overcome the unfair twenty-two pounds he gave *Noor over the mile and one-quarter. He ran a fantastic race, only one and one-quarter lengths separating him from *Noor at the wire, and he forced *Noor to set a new track record.

The San Juan Capistrano Handicap was a repeat performance. *Noor had a weight advantage of thirteen pounds for the one and three-quarter mile race and Citation came in second by a nose. *Noor did it, and he set a new American track record in the process. It was the greatest race ever run at Santa Anita. No one ever forgot the last quarter of a mile when *Noor and Citation pounded down the track shoulder to shoulder.

Citation and Calumet had been going through a series of frustrations in trying to pass Stymie's money record, but slowly the Calumet contender inched his way up to Stymie's $911,355. Citation had stopped racing as a three year old less than $50,000 away from the goal, and his first six California races as a five year old brought him within $1,275 of the top.

In the Golden Gate Mile, a handicap, he passed Stymie's record and became the world's leading money winner. Carrying 128 pounds, he set a new world record at 1:33$\frac{3}{5}$. It was a fantastic race.

The *Noor-Citation competition went on for two more races, the Forty-Niners and the Golden Gate Handicap. *Noor won them both but, again, had to set a world's record in each to do so.

The Calumet Comet's five-year-old year was notably frustrating. He had raced nine times, won twice, and had seven seconds. Although he won only one of his last six races, a new record was set in each.

After the Golden Gate in June 1950, Citation went home to Calumet to rest. In January 1951, as a six year old, he returned to California and ran badly in three short races, finishing third twice and fifth once. A second and two firsts in his next races brought him to within $14,240 of Calumet's million dollar and final goal.

The Hollywood Gold Cup, one and one-quarter miles, guaranteed $100,000 to the winner. Citation, for the first time in California, received a break in the weights and carried 120 pounds. One of Calumet's great fillies, Bull Lea's Bewitch, was weighted at 108, while a son of Count Fleet, Be Fleet, was handicapped at 122 pounds. Citation finished first. Although he cooled out sound, Mrs. Wright decided it was time to retire the Calumet Comet as the world's first equine millionaire.

RACING RECORD

Year	Age	Starts	1st	2nd	3rd	Earnings
1947	2	9	8	1	0	$ 155,680
1948	3	20	19	1	0	709,470
1949	4	0	0	0	0	......
1950	5	9	2	7	0	73,480
1951	6	7	3	1	2	147,130
	Totals	45	32	10	2	$1,085,760

In his four-year racing career, Citation started forty-five times—winning thirty-two, with ten seconds, two thirds, and one fifth. He won $1,085,760, but his two and three-year-old years had been fantastic. In twenty-nine starts he finished second twice and won all the rest.

A few years later when Ben Jones was asked about his favorite, Citation, he said, "There is nothing a horse could have that Citation did not have. A horse could not come any greater. I do not believe there has ever been a horse greater than Citation, in any century."

Citation was retired to stud but he did not have the prepotency of his sire, Bull Lea. It is a strange quirk of genetics that Bull Lea, a fair race horse, was one of the greatest sires of all time, while Citation, the greatest of the great, was an indifferent sire.

Citation had started his three-year-old year at Miami's Hialeah, and in 1965 a statue of Citation was unveiled by the former Mrs. Wright, now Mrs. Gene Markey. Eddie Arcaro and Jimmy Jones were both there to see their favorite, sculptured in bronze, standing on a green Carrara marble base in the midst of a lily pond. Sculptured in Florence, it was a fitting life-size likeness of a greater than life-size horse.

On August 8, 1970, Citation, aged twenty-five, died at Calumet. He was buried in the Calumet graveyard at the foot of Bull Lea's statue and, as one looks at his grave, Ben Jones's words come to mind. "Citation was the greatest of them all . . . I've tried to fault him but I just can't find any holes. He's the best. Maybe we'll never see his likes again in our time."

Citation had everything—including an English bull dog buddy, Bushel.

Epilogue

AFTER CITATION, it took twenty-five years to produce another Triple Crown winner—Secretariat. Citation, although a superhorse, was the best of a mere 5,000 foals registered with The Jockey Club in 1945. Secretariat had to be the fastest of 25,000 youngsters foaled in 1970. The number of thoroughbreds born each year is continually on the increase, and so are the odds against winning a Triple Crown; the next wearer may have to be the best of 35,000 or more youngsters.

State governments, hungry for tax dollars, are encouraging the expansion of racing. New tracks are being built, legislation is being passed for flat racing at night and on Sundays, and for longer racing seasons. The New York Racing Association meetings have been extended to December 31, bringing some winter racing to New York City. This expansion will further increase the demand for horses, and the breeding industry will supply that need.

With more and more races to fill, the temptation will be even greater to race two-year-olds too young and too often, breaking down many a Triple Crown prospect before his three-year-old year.

In 1973, Secretariat and his equally photogenic owner, Penny Tweedy, brought magnificent racing into millions of American homes, and their success gave the pleasure-horse explosion an added boost. Horse shows, combined training events, and pony-club-sponsored activities are booming. More and more thoroughbreds, not fast enough to race, are finding a new way of life as show and field hunters, jumpers, event horses, and even as pleasure hacks.

As thousands of youngsters, boys and girls, become good riders, many will look toward the race track for jobs with horses. Today, exercise girls outnumber the men. Women jockeys, starting with Kathy Kusner of international horse show fame, are beginning to make their mark. The stunning Robyn Smith rides winners at New York's Aqueduct—the Big A—and more women will doubtless follow in her footsteps.

To date, no one has given serious consideration to a filly's winning, or to a woman's riding, a Triple Crown winner. But the 1970s have seen a remarkable group of fillies racing, and expert women jockeys riding, on both sides of the Atlantic. If this continues, the next Triple Crown winner may well be a filly—groomed, exercised, trained, and ridden by women.

It could take another twenty-five years—or more—to find a new wearer of the Triple Crown. The Kentucky Derby, the Preakness, and the Belmont are the three necessary stops on the road to fame and fortune for the owner, the trainer, and the rider. For the best colt or filly of that unknown year, the reward, as always, will be equine immortality.

Glossary

* Denotes horse foaled abroad and imported into the United States, as *Sir Gallahad III or *Blenheim II.

AGE. Every thoroughbred has, by custom, the same birthday, January first. For racing purposes he becomes one year older on New Year's Day regardless of the date he was foaled.

BLINKERS. A hood fitting over horse's head with leather or plastic cups restricting horse's side vision. Used at trainer's discretion if his horse is distracted by those alongside.

COLORS—HORSES

Bay, Brown or Black. Various shades from light brown to black. Overlapping colors are very difficult to distinguish and depend on expert classification. In all cases there is a black mane and tail.

Chestnut. Copper colored, with shadings from light yellow to a liver brown. Never has a black mane or tail.

Gray. A mixture of white and black hairs. Foals are born very dark, almost black, and turn lighter. Many turn completely white with age.

Roan. A mixture of white and chestnut or bay hairs.

COLORS—RACING SILKS. Distinctive jacket and cap, formerly of silk, now made of synthetic cloth, in varicolored design. Owner chooses a pattern which must be approved and registered by The Jockey Club. First used at Newmarket, England, in 1700s.

COLT. Young male horse, four years old or less.

COOLING OUT. A horse undergoes enormous physical exertion during a race and, like any athlete, "cools out" after the contest. He is washed down, covered with a light wool blanket, a "cooler," if the temperature warrants, and led until he has stopped sweating and his heartbeat and respiration have returned to normal. A person who walks a race horse during this period is a "hot walker."

The strains and stresses on a horse's legs become apparent after he is "cooled out." Many animals hurt themselves running, but give no indication of injury until after they are relaxed. Every trainer waits anxiously, to see if his horse "cools out sound," with no apparent disability.

DAM. The female parent of a horse.

DOPE. Racing involves big money, especially in the betting, and the temptation to "fix" a horse has been present for hundreds of years.

Slowing down a horse is easy—a feed or a bucket of water just before a race makes a great difference in his performance. Drugs, of course, are the most common depressants and stimulants.

There was a drug problem in the early days of racing but, since the 1930s, stringent enforcement of anti-doping rules by the racing commissions of the various states (involving testing of the horse's urine and saliva after a race) has virtually eliminated drugging.

Since the 1960s, another problem has arisen as a result of the enormous number and sophistication of new drugs. Although hard drugs have virtually disappeared, the use of hormones, tranquilizers, massive injections of vitamins, and of analgesics (pain killers which are not narcotic), has opened a whole new area of controversy.

In 1968 Dancer's Image came in first in the Kentucky Derby. When a trace of Butazolidin (also known as "Bute"), an analgesic with the effect of aspirin, was found in his urine, it resulted in the disqualification of Dancer's Image and the beginning of years of lawsuits.

There is, at the moment, much controversy as to whether the rules should be modified to permit the use of these non-hard drugs.

FAVORITE. Horse most favored to win, determined by lowest odds.

FILLY. Young female horse, four years old or less.

FOAL. A young horse, less than one year old.

To foal. For a broodmare to give birth to a foal.

FURLONG. One eighth of a mile, from old English expression "a furrow long"—the length of a plowed field.

GATE. Starting gate: metal structure on wheels, placed at starting point and towed off immediately afterwards. Contains side-by-side stalls with doors at front and back of each stall. Horses enter from rear and the doors are closed manually behind them. The front gates are simultaneously opened electrically, ensuring an even start.

GELDING. A male horse who has been surgically altered by castration.

GET. The collective offspring of a stallion.

HAND. A horse's height, from the ground to the highest point of the withers (the hump over the shoulders), is measured in hands and inches. Each hand is four inches, so that a height of 16:2 is 16 hands two inches or a total of 66 inches.

HANDICAP. See *Races*

HORSE. In thoroughbred racing terminology, a male five years old or more.

IN THE MONEY. The purse is usually split among the first four horses, so a horse is *in the money* if he finishes among the first four.

MAIDEN. A horse that has never won a race. "To break his maiden"—to win for the first time—is a phrase also used for a jockey's first win.

MARE. A female horse at least five years old.

Broodmare. A mare who has become a mother.

MUTUEL OR PARI-MUTUEL. System of betting in which all money bet on each race at track is pooled. State and track first get a percentage "off the top," and the remainder is mathematically split among bettors on first three finishers.

PADDOCK. Saddling and mounting area of track.

PHOTO FINISH. A close finish in which the judges use an ingenious system of photography utilizing a continuous strip of film, moving behind an open slit in rear of camera lens to determine the placing of the horses.

PLATER. A horse that runs in claiming races.

POST POSITION. Horse's position in starting gate, counting outward from inside rail. Places are determined by lot, after entries close, the day before the race.

PURSE. The monetary prize for a race. Derived from the 1700s when prize money was put into a silk purse and hung at the finish to be "taken down" by the winner.

RACE. Webster calls it "a competition of speed, as in running." This definition is true, but oversimplified for horse racing.

To afford variety, the tracks offer infinite combinations of requirements for each race. The entries can be restricted by sex or by age. In addition, the horses' performances can be equalized by the weight assigned them (by a "handicapper"). The more weight a horse carries, the slower he runs. The old rule of thumb, for races one mile or more, is that every additional pound of weight will cause a horse to finish one length further back.

There are hundreds of combinations of conditions for entry, from the Triple Crown races, which are simply for three year olds at 126 pounds, to other more complicated requirements.

The purpose of various conditions for entry is to equalize the competition and keep the bettors interested and guessing—for the success of racing all comes down to the enthusiasm of the bettor at the mutuel window. Ultimately, he pays the bill.

The principal types of races referred to in this book are the following:

Allowance Race. Race in which weight to be carried by each horse is decided by his past performances. The formula varies, but usually the weight each horse will carry for the race is determined by the amount of money and/or number of races the horse has won during a specified time.

Claiming Race. Race in which each horse entered is subject to purchase. For example, in a $5,000 claiming race any horse entered can be "claimed"—or purchased—for the claiming price stated, by any owner who has started a horse in that particular race meeting.

Futurity. A race for two-year-olds, in which entries are made when the horse is still a foal.

Handicap Race. Unlike an allowance race, where a mathematical formula is used to determine the weight a horse will carry, the weights for a handicap race are assigned at the sole discretion of the racing secretary of the track. Based completely on his individual judgment of each horse's ability, he assigns more weight to the faster horses. The racing secretary's dream is to be clever enough to have all the horses finish in a dead heat.

Stakes Race. From "Sweepstakes." Unlike other races in which there is no entry fee, each owner starting a horse in a stakes race must put up a nominating fee, an entry fee, and a starting fee. To the total of all fees received, the track adds an amount, sometimes in excess of $100,000, which is the *Added Money*. In most stakes races all fees received from owners go to the winning horse, together with a major share of the Added Money.

Weight-for-Age Race. Determined by the "Scale of Weights"— a tabulation setting weights based on a horse's age, the distance of the race, and the time of year when run.

SEASON. A mare is "in season" at the time when her mating to a stallion is most likely to produce a foal.

SERVICE. The act of sexual intercourse between a stallion and a mare.

SIRE. The male parent of a horse. A *foundation sire* is a horse who has passed on running ability to a long line of descendants.

SPLINT. An enlargement of the bone of the leg causing lameness in the horse, usually temporary.

STALLION. A male horse who has not been castrated.

STANDARDBRED. A horse bred to light harness horse standards; trotters and pacers who race while pulling a sulky, as opposed to the thoroughbred galloping with jockey.

STRETCH

Homestretch. Straightaway leading to the finish.

Backstretch. Straightaway on opposite side of track from finish line—also used to designate the stable area.

STUD. A group of horses kept for breeding purposes.

Stand at Stud. A stallion available for breeding is "standing at stud."

Stud Book. The official registry of the pedigree of every thoroughbred. The English and American stud books are kept by the Jockey Clubs of each country.

SYNDICATE. A partnership to purchase a horse. The total price is divided into shares and subscribed to by a number of people.

THOROUGHBRED. A horse whose ancestry can be traced back to one of the three founding sires imported into England from North Africa and the Near East: the Byerly Turk, the Godolphin Arabian, or the Darley Arabian.

In all cases descent is through one of their sons:

Eclipse—foaled in 1764, the year of the Great Eclipse of the sun—great-great-grandson of the Darley Arabian.

Matchem—foaled in 1748, a grandson of the Godolphin Arabian.

Herod—foaled in 1758, a great-great-grandson of the Byerly Turk.

TRAINER. The person who reaps the credit, or more often the blame, for a horse's performance. In preparing the horse, the trainer makes virtually every decision—from the feeding and amount or type of work between races to the choice of a jockey and the strategy for a given race.

Public Trainer. A trainer for a number of owners who charges per horse for board and expenses, and receives a share of the winnings.

Private Trainer. Works for one owner, usually for yearly salary and share of purses. Owner pays all expenses.

WEANLING. A young horse who is separated from its mother toward the end of the first year.

WEIGHING IN. Jockey, and all equipment, is *weighed out* before the race to ensure that correct weight is being carried. After finish, jockey is *weighed in* before the race is official.

WEIGHT. Predetermined weight that each horse must carry in a race, made up of jockey, saddle, and other equipment. Deficiency in weight is remedied by a pad of canvas or leather, with a series of pockets containing lead slabs weighing one pound each. This is placed over horse's back under the saddle. If the jockey cannot make the weight, he is allowed to ride, but at not more than five pounds overweight.

WINDED. A "winded" horse has a diminished ability to breathe. This results from a partial paralysis of the larynx which constricts portion of airway; therefore horse gasps for breath while galloping. Quite common, particularly among large horses.

YEARLING. After its first New Year's Day birthday, the weanling becomes a yearling.

Index